"Marcia Reynolds gives leaders the tools they need to go beyond basic coaching. Both provocative and practical, she lays out a framework for getting to the heart of the matter in conversations and includes vibrant case studies to ensure you apply what you learn."

—Jennifer B. Kahnweiler, PhD, author of *Quiet Influence*

"This book leaves leaders and coaches no excuse for avoiding difficult issues. It's time we all go beyond our comfort zones to do our best work."

—Prof. Konstantin Korotov, PhD, Director, Center for Leadership Development Research, European School of Management and Technology, Berlin, Germany

"*The Discomfort Zone* presents valuable techniques to harness friction, break down limiting perspectives, and create shifts in thinking. I learned how to constructively challenge my team by expanding their minds and facilitating growth. You won't seek being comfortable again!"

—Bettina Hein, founder and CEO, Pixability

"In *The Discomfort Zone*, Marcia Reynolds clearly describes how leaders can be most effective in communicating and coaching their teams to greater success even in the most stressful situations."

—Victor F. Trastek, MD, Emeritus CEO, Mayo Clinic in Arizona, and Associate Director, Professionalism and Leadership, Mayo Clinic

"They say leaders make lemonade out of lemons; with *The Discomfort Zone*, you can turn conflict into career wins!"

—Jeffrey Hayzlett, show host, Bloomberg TV; bestselling author of *The Mirror Test* and *Running the Gauntlet*; and sometime cowboy

"Marcia Reynolds shows us that it is time to quit diffusing difficult conversations and embrace them. She guides us to use our head, heart, and gut to create the learning and growth needed to foster an innovative environment with engaged employees."

—Betty-Ann Heggie, former Senior Vice President, Potash Corporation, and member of Canada's Top 100 Most Powerful Women Hall of Fame

"No one has approached leadership conversations like this author. She gives her reader a clear path to progress. Don't just read and nod at the ideas here; put them to work immediately."

—Beverly Kaye, founder of Career Systems International and bestselling coauthor of *Love 'Em or Lose 'Em*

"This supremely practical book will guide you to help others move beyond their resistance. As you develop the confidence to embrace challenging interactions you'll liberate tremendous creative energy and become a more effective leader at work and at home."

—**Michael J. Gelb, bestselling author of *How to Think Like Leonardo da Vinci* and *Creativity on Demand***

"Dr. Reynolds helps us go beyond just 'getting through' difficult conversations. A master coach, she synthesizes the deepest wisdom from neuroscience and leadership to give us something really *useful*. This will be my new go-to guide for leaders."

—**Madeleine Homan Blanchard, cofounder of Coaching Services and CD2 Leadership, The Ken Blanchard Companies**

"Marcia Reynolds shows how the 'discomfort zone' provides the fastest path for helping others fulfill their potential. Her brilliant book is a guide for leaders at all levels to make a real difference."

—**Jesse Lyn Stoner, coauthor of *Full Steam Ahead!***

"Marcia Reynolds reveals the thought processes and techniques used by masterful coaches to engage others in transformational conversations. If you're looking to take your coaching capabilities to the next level, *The Discomfort Zone* will prove an insightful and invaluable guide."

—**Dianna Anderson, CEO, Cylient, and coauthor of *Coaching That Counts***

"*The Discomfort Zone* provides solid practices for making challenging conversations a powerful tool for helping others learn, perform, and excel."

—**Chip R. Bell, coauthor of *Managers as Mentors***

"It's crazy-making for leaders when they can't communicate with their people. They need to enter the discomfort zone where real connections take place, creating the possibility for breakthrough conversations."

—**Darelyn "DJ" Mitsch, President, Pyramid Resource Group, and author of *Team Advantage* and *Zombies to Zealots***

The Discomfort Zone

The Discomfort Zone

*How Leaders Turn
Difficult Conversations
into Breakthroughs*

Marcia Reynolds

Berrett–Koehler Publishers, Inc.
San Francisco
a BK Business book

Berrett-Koehler Publishers, Inc.
235 Montgomery Street, Suite 650
San Francisco, CA 94104-2916
Tel: (415) 288-0260   Fax: (415) 362-2512   www.bkconnection.com

Ordering Information

Quantity sales. Special discounts are available on quantity purchases by corporations, associations, and others. For details, contact the "Special Sales Department" at the Berrett-Koehler address above.

Individual sales. Berrett-Koehler publications are available through most bookstores. They can also be ordered directly from Berrett-Koehler: Tel: (800) 929-2929; Fax: (802) 864-7626; www.bkconnection.com

Orders for college textbook/course adoption use. Please contact Berrett-Koehler: Tel: (800) 929-2929; Fax: (802) 864-7626.

Orders by U.S. trade bookstores and wholesalers. Please contact Ingram Publisher Services, Tel: (800) 509-4887; Fax: (800) 838-1149; E-mail: customer.service@ingrampublisherservices.com; or visit www.ingrampublisherservices.com/Ordering for details about electronic ordering.

Berrett-Koehler and the BK logo are registered trademarks of Berrett-Koehler Publishers, Inc.

Printed in the United States of America

Berrett-Koehler books are printed on long-lasting acid-free paper. When it is available, we choose paper that has been manufactured by environmentally responsible processes. These may include using trees grown in sustainable forests, incorporating recycled paper, minimizing chlorine in bleaching, or recycling the energy produced at the paper mill.

Library of Congress Cataloging-in-Publication Data
Reynolds, Marcia.
The discomfort zone : how leaders turn difficult conversations into breakthroughs / Marcia Reynolds. -- First Edition.
    pages cm
    Summary: "Leaders, coaches, and mentors are charged with helping others to stretch their limits. However, few people enjoy hearing the messy--and sometimes painful--feedback it takes to overcome a personal obstacle. Marcia Reynolds shows how to use the discomfort zone to help others grow, not suffer"-- Provided by publisher.
    ISBN 978-1-62656-065-9 (paperback)
    1. Leadership. 2. Personal coaching. 3. Mentoring. 4. Oral communication. I. Title.
    HD57.7.R494 2014
    658.3'124--dc23
                                                                              2014017439
First Edition
19 18 17 16 15 14   10 9 8 7 6 5 4 3 2 1

Interior design and project management: Dovetail Publishing Services
Cover design: Wes Youssi, M.80 Design   Author photo (page 163): Tina Celle

Contents

Introduction

What Is Good about Discomfort?

The Discomfort Zone is the moment of uncertainty when people are most open to learning.

On the day I resigned from my last corporate position, one of the vice presidents came into my office and said, "You can't go. Who will I talk to?" I recalled our first heated encounter five years earlier when he was the head of quality and I was the touchy-feely new girl hired to make the employees feel better about the changes that were happening in the organization. We were aliens from two different worlds. Yet together, we created a program that seeded the cultural transformation that helped the organization become the top performing IPO (initial public offering) in the United States in 1993.

There were many conversations in which I challenged his beliefs about what motivates people, questioned his views on leadership, dug into the source of his emotions when he no longer wanted to put up with me, and helped him see that letting go of some of his habits and perspectives would help him achieve what he knew was possible for the company. At times, he didn't like me, but he came to trust me, even when I was wrong. I learned a lot, too, about the business and what it takes to transform both one leader and an organization. We both became surprisingly comfortable with uncomfortable conversations.

His remorse over losing our regular conversations inspired me to be formally trained as a coach. I also pursued a degree in organizational psychology so I could codify and improve what I found works in coaching to shift someone's viewpoint when the conversation feels difficult. I have been coached by masters when I had my defenses broken down with one statement and had to wait for my brain to reorganize and make sense of the new perspective. I have taught and mentored leaders around the world to use the skills for themselves to create breakthrough moments in their conversations. I found that leaders who master the skills of helping others think through their blind spots, attachments, and resistance are not only effective, but they are also the most remembered and revered.

In the book *Synchronicity*, Joseph Jaworski said the most successful leaders are those who participate in helping others create new realities.[1] The leader engages in conversations that bring to light a person's filters and frames. When the factors that frame the meaning of a situation are revealed, the view of what is true changes and becomes clear.

A change in the view of what is true is needed for long-lasting and positive change. To do this, you have to be comfortable with disruption and tension in a conversation, creating a Discomfort Zone in which new ideas are birthed. A leader who uses the Discomfort Zone emphasizes potential rather than problems.

What Is the Discomfort Zone?

In order to define who we are and make sense of the world around us, our brains develop constructs and rules that we strongly protect without much thought. Neuroscientist Michael Gazzaniga says we get stuck in our automatic thought-processing and fool ourselves into thinking we are acting consciously and willfully.[2] "Our conscious awareness is the mere tip of the iceberg of nonconscious processing," Gazzaniga says.[3] When someone asks you why you did something, you immediately come up with an ad hoc answer that fits the situation even if the response doesn't make complete sense. These quick interpretations actually constrain the brain, making human beings narrow-minded by nature.

To help people think differently, you have to disturb the automatic processing.[4] This is best done by challenging the beliefs that created the frames and surfacing the underlying fears, needs, and desires that are keeping the constructs in place. There needs to be a hole in the *force field* that protects their sense of reality before they will actively explore, examine, and change their beliefs and behavior.

People need to be aroused by surprising statements about their behavior and by questions that make them stop and think about what they are saying. If you break through their mental frames, they will stare at you for a moment as their brains look for ways to make sense of what they are considering. Then a burst of adrenaline could cause an emotional reaction, anything from nervous laughter to anger before an insight emerges. If you act on this moment by helping to solidify the new awareness, their minds will change. If you do not facilitate this process, a strong ego may work backward to justify the previous behavior.[5]

The Discomfort Zone is the moment of uncertainty when people are most open to learning. An emotional reaction occurs at this moment indicating a chance for the person to develop a new perspective, see a different solution to the problem, and potentially grow as a person. Joshua Fields Millburn and Ryan Nicodemus, authors of *Minimalism: Live a Meaningful Life*, define this moment as feeling temporarily naked. "Because when you're naked, you're most vulnerable. And when you're vulnerable, that's when radical growth happens."[6]

Because emotions are involved, the discomfort can be felt by both people in the conversation. The leader or coach's discomfort is secondary to the process, however, and might not even exist with practice. For true shifts in thinking and behavior to occur, you must be willing to challenge a person's beliefs, interrupt his patterns, and short-circuit the conviction to his logic even when it feels uncomfortable. This is a Discomfort Zone conversation.

There is a range of possible reactions when you do this. The realization could be minimal, with the person responding, "Oh, yeah, I see what you mean." On the other end of the spectrum, a person could gasp with embarrassment and then beg for time to think about what occurred, especially if previous behavior has been destructive and he or she did not recognize the impact until that moment. Many times people will laugh at themselves; they might even get angry when it is difficult for them to accept the truth.

Consider your own experiences. The sudden, new, and amazing solution to a problem probably didn't come to you as you hovered over your desk rearranging the details. The truth about your future didn't appear to you as you sat in the dark ruminating over past conversations. Profound changes to your personal and professional life weren't caused by a self-generated flash of insight. The sudden solution, amazing truth, and profound understanding that gave you no choice but to change your mind most likely came as a result of a disruptive question and deep reflection initiated by someone else.

For the same reason you can't tickle yourself, you can't fully explore your own thoughts. Your brain will block and desensitize you to self-imposed exploration. When someone you trust adeptly challenges your reasoning and asks you the powerful question that breaks down your protective frame, your brain is forced to reorder data in your long-term memory. For a moment, the breakdown feels awkward. You might feel a pinch of anger or sadness, but then you are just as likely to laugh at what you see . . . after you gasp. There must be an emotional stake in the game for restructuring to occur.

This book first shows how you set the foundation. There must be a level of trust and safety so the person will not think you are being manipulative. Then it will show how to use positive confrontation, honest feedback, and frame-shattering questions to spark activity in the brain causing changes in perception, self-image, and behavior. The reward goes beyond getting good results to experiencing deep fulfillment when you witness the human before you make this mind-altering shift.

The Best Times to Have a Discomfort Zone Conversation

Picture yourself sitting in a conversation with a woman you know is smart and committed to her work, but she is complaining about a situation and feels stuck with no solution and she is resisting the changes others have told her to make. Maybe you are wondering why she can't see what's best for her. You want her to quit focusing on the problem. You want her to try something new. You want her to move on. You've given her feedback. She discounts your view. You've suggested solutions but the conversation just circles back to what is not working. This is a perfect time for a Discomfort Zone conversation!

You can also use these skills to engage and retain your top talent. A bad economy can mask employee dissatisfaction. As soon as the economy shows some stability, people begin to look elsewhere for jobs, especially the high achievers. They spend a good portion of their attention and time looking for their next opportunity, maybe with a competitor.

When economies thrive, employee engagement is critical to retain top talent and meet increasing demand for production and innovation. I remember how successful headhunters were in the booming 90s when we were losing our top engineers to the better paying companies down the street. Fortunately, many returned when they realized the culture down the street was not as caring and inspiring as we were working to create.

A good way of retaining top talent is to listen to them, trust they can figure things out, and provide development opportunities, which include expanding their minds as well as their skills. A survey published in *Harvard Business Review* found that although young high achievers were given high-visibility jobs and increasing responsibilities, they were dissatisfied with the lack of mentoring and coaching they received.[7] There seems to be a gap in what management thinks and what employees want, indicating that leaders aren't listening.

Clearly, leaders need to spend more time with their top talent, helping them think through problems, see situations more strategically, and grow beyond their limitations. *The Discomfort Zone* will give you these skills.

What You Will Get from Reading This Book

In this book the word *leader* will apply to anyone engaged in a conversation who is focused on expanding the awareness of a person or group of people. You may be a leader, change agent, colleague, inside coach, outside coach, or consultant.

The word *person* will apply to the human you are speaking with no matter the nature of the relationship. When engaging in these conversations, perception of status should not get in the way. The person you are with is not a protégé, direct report, or student. He or she must feel you are an equal partner in the journey. How to ensure that someone feels your respect will be explored in Chapter Two.

Chapter One will look at how *The Discomfort Zone* is different from other conversation and coaching techniques and when these conversations are most useful. The techniques aren't a cure-all for every dilemma because certain criteria must be met to have the intended effect. Chapter One will explore what conditions are necessary to support a successful outcome.

When you begin your conversation, there are necessary steps you must take to establish trust and positive intention so when you provoke discomfort, both short- and long-term results are constructive. Chapter Two gives guidelines for creating this safety bubble to effectively use the Discomfort Zone.

Chapters Three and Four describe the steps and provide examples for giving honest feedback, using reflective and informative statements, and asking powerful questions to break down barriers and broaden awareness. The skill development includes methods for observing your internal processing and protection systems as well as hearing these systems operate in others. You will learn how to listen from the three processing centers of your neural network—your head, heart, and gut—while staying present to the person you are with.

Chapters Five and Six bring together the approaches explained in case studies so you can better implement what you have read. Chapter Five looks at how to break through well-established defense routines that are keeping people from making changes or handling situations in the most productive way. Chapter Six explores cases in which the leader helped people work through blocks to realize more potent ways to apply their strengths and passion.

Chapter Seven is designed to support you as you implement the skills. It will provide resources and practices that will help you feel both comfortable and competent when having Discomfort Zone conversations. You will also find ways for finding and creating communities where you can share cases, practice together, and build on the insights this book offers.

Effective leaders help others think more broadly for themselves. The more leaders can get the neurons sparking, the greater the chance for innovation, unexpected achievement, and the continuous desire to grow. On the practical side, you will see more engagement and retention, positively impacting the bottom-line results. On the human side, the outcome is more fulfilling, for you, too, as you come to appreciate the power of these conversations. *The Discomfort Zone* will give you the means for creating provocative conversations in which you, those you work with, and possibly your entire organization will experience a brave, new workplace built on unbridled curiosity.

Chapter One

Criteria for Choosing a Discomfort Zone Conversation

"The function of leadership is to produce more leaders, not more followers."
Ralph Nader, from *Crashing the Party*

I was sharing my latest complaints about my peers with my boss when he suddenly sighed so loudly I stopped mid-sentence. When he had my attention, he said, "I know you work hard. I know you want the best for the company, but everybody seems to let you down. Is anyone ever good enough for you?"

I sat paralyzed for a dreadfully long time. When I finally exhaled, the tension rolled down my shoulders resting heavily in my legs. I felt both embarrassed and amazed. My coach had once made a similar observation after my rant about my dating fiascos. Here was my *wall of protection* showing up again at work. All I could say was, "Of course. You're right." I knew I would never see my work relationships the same again.

The question my boss asked me led me to recognize a pattern of behavior that kept me from fully engaging with my team members to resolve problems. I am a high achiever. I did good work on my own and felt snubbed the moment I wasn't recognized for my accomplishments or grand ideas. To ease the pain, I found reasons to complain about how others were not living up to their promises or expectations. Instead of learning how I could influence more effectively or realize even grander results with others, I focused on highlighting their flaws.

Whether my boss knew all of this or not, he had asked me the perfect question that disrupted my pattern of thinking and forced me to reflect on what I was saying. If he had told me what I was doing instead of asking the question, I would have resisted his allegation. No matter how clear and targeted were his comments, his words of wisdom and advice would have hit the automatic reject button in my brain.

It wasn't just the powerful question that had such a profound effect on me. His timing was impeccable. I felt he heard me. He was responding to my story, not practicing a technique. I was amazed, uncomfortable, and a bit embarrassed but I didn't feel judged. He had masterfully moved me into the Discomfort Zone. My sense of *who I thought I was* changed forever.

I share this example to help clarify what using the Discomfort Zone is in practice and, more importantly, what it is not. Using the Discomfort Zone is not the same as initiating a challenging conversation. The process is based on a specific type of coaching most useful when it is clear that a shift in perception and self-awareness would be helpful to the person you are with as he or she stumbles through a perplexing situation. You choose the Discomfort Zone when you want to *assist others in thinking differently.*

Not Another Conversation Book

You may have read one or many of the books teaching how to hold challenging, courageous, fierce, crucial, real, and authentic conversations. You may have a favorite; mine is *Authentic Conversations.*[1]

These books are important. They teach leaders how to better approach a conversation about difficult issues they need to address.

These conversation books focus *on the speaker*. They provide direction on how a person can best deliver a message and achieve an outcome for themselves. There might be a mutual benefit, but the primary target is helping the person who speaks first.

This is where *The Discomfort Zone* differs. The focus shifts *to the receiver*, the person you are speaking with. You don't have a message to deliver; you desire someone to expand his awareness to see his situation and himself in a different light. You don't tell him what you want. You want him to discover, create, or unveil this new reality on his own. In short, you want him to think for himself. You are the facilitator of this process.

You might be thinking, *Why bother?* Most corporations honor those with a no-nonsense, frank, get-to-the-point approach. The leader who is respectful yet firm keeps the engines running. Straight talk and efficiency are requisites in a competitive marketplace.

Yes, using direct, candid talk can alleviate inefficiencies, hold people accountable for their goals, and align people around clear expectations. There may be negative reactions, but the sting is brief if they see value in the solution and in their contribution. As the authors say in the book *Crucial Conversations*, the goal is to "Be persuasive, not abrasive."[2] There are times you will choose to have these types of conversations.

Even when done well, though, when the focus of a conversation is on what the leader wants, a breakthrough in perception won't be achieved. The receiver might agree. Problem solving might be satisfactory. Incremental shifts in behavior might occur, but the opportunity to cause a mind-changing tilt in perception that allows the person to see a situation in an entirely new light is lost. If, as Ralph Nader said, "The function of leadership is to produce more leaders,"[3] then any conversation that starts with the leader declaring the way forward misses the mark.

If instead you believe the person you are with is capable of seeing things differently and finding new solutions with a little help thinking it through, you are likely to get better results if you act more as a "thinking partner" than a holder of the truth. You may want the person to change his point of view, but you facilitate the shifts in thinking through questions and reflective statements instead of by telling him your desires and opinions. You may feel you have less control in these conversations—at least until you become more comfortable with the process—but the outcomes are worth the effort.

How This Approach Differs from Traditional Leadership Coaching Techniques

Coaching has become a recognized leadership skill over the past decade. Leaders who coach are more adept at triggering people's imagination and creative thinking skills. Using an inquiry approach has proven to engage people more fully at physical, mental, and emotional levels. However, much of the coach training for leaders falls short of producing breakthrough results.

Traditionally, coach training for leaders teaches how to be supportive, encouraging, inquisitive, and nonjudgmental. Most approaches are appreciative, helping people build on their strengths instead of focusing on their weaknesses. Solutions are often creative. People feel heartened instead of defeated.

These approaches are useful but often not enough when dealing with bright, ambitious people with disparate, strong opinions.[4] Challenging assumptions and raising uncomfortable questions promote critical thinking. Discomfort Zone conversations start by building trust and rapport, but then the conversations go deeper to create the possibility for a breakthrough in thinking.

Most strong-willed people respect someone who stands up to their resistance, and then asks them the questions that provoke them to scrutinize what they do. In a recent interview, world-renowned coach Sir John Whitmore said, "I think that was how it was when coaching began, being gentle and supportive. But I think under today's circumstances this is changing."

Many leaders and coaches are not trained or courageous enough to use discomfort to create breakthroughs. Whitmore added, "I personally like being challenged. I have a couple of coaches who coach with a scalpel and I love it." To break through the barriers and address protective thinking habits, you must be willing to hold a balance of pressure and care in the conversation. You can't avoid challenge if you want people to see the world around them in a revolutionary way."

Also, many leaders and coaches are trained to quickly shift the person from feeling negative to positive, going away from the problem to what is possible. If this happens early in the conversation, the person might feel ashamed for continuing to feel angry or frustrated during or after the conversation. His or her real needs remain unspoken.

When working with the Discomfort Zone, you may trigger negative emotions, which is a good sign. When a person realizes she has blocked a truth that was in her face the entire time, she may feel mortified, angry, or sad. As explained in the Introduction, these emotions indicate learning is occurring. You have broken through a protective barrier in the brain. The person is finally confronting her rationalizations or seeing her blind spots. Because of this, a clearer and broader understanding of the situation can emerge.

The goal is to break through a person's guise of *knowing*. When people face a surprising revelation about their behavior, they will pause and then react. Malcolm Gladwell quoted psychologist Joshua Aronson in *Blink* saying, "People are ignorant of the things that affect their action, yet they rarely feel ignorant."[5] The reaction to bringing these things to light will register somewhere between slight discomfort and an emotional outpour. These reactions indicate their mental frames are restructuring, clearing the way for people to see what is truly driving their behavior when they couldn't see this before. Creating this discomfort gives people a chance to evaluate their experiences.[6] The truth can hurt or at least surprise before it sets people free.

Using the Discomfort Zone teaches leadership coaching methods that include the means to create trust as well as the ability to challenge and expand a person's thinking. In the process, the leader remains nonjudgmental and caring so the person feels safe enough to express a range of emotions as his or her brain recognizes something unexpected. This is how leaders create learning environments that improve productivity, innovation, and leadership bench strength.

Timing and Purpose

There are times when the methods taught in this book may be inappropriate for a specific situation. The best times to employ the techniques are when the person is having interpersonal/communications issues or motivational blocks and when you are helping someone develop decision-making and leadership capabilities. Even in these scenarios, specific circumstances must be present to have the intended effect.

The Right Time to Choose
the Discomfort Zone

A common leadership misperception is if someone isn't perform-ing well, he doesn't know what he is doing and needs to be told what action to take. Nothing is more annoying than being told how to do something you already know. If you have been doing this to someone, you may be the source of his dwindling motiva-tion. The choice to tell, teach, or advise someone should not be taken lightly.

Seek to discover what he already knows and is capable of doing. Then if you both determine company or project knowl-edge is needed, you can share what you know or provide resources. If skills are wanting, you can pinpoint what specific training will help.

Most likely, the competent person you are speaking to doesn't need knowledge or training; he needs your support in expanding his view around an issue and in understanding the impact of his behavior and decisions. These needs are the perfect criteria for using the Discomfort Zone. Start by understanding what he knows and then seek to discover what gap in perception or emotional block is keeping him from seeing a plausible solu-tion. When the person has sufficient skills and knowledge, you will be more successful when you energize him using *what he knows* than to exhaust him with *what you know*.

Your Belief in the Person's Potential

The conversation must be based on your belief in the person's potential to grow. Ask yourself the following question: "Is it more important that the conversation is about discovering how he or she is able to work best or that I steer the ship so goals are achieved?" If you believe in the latter, it is more likely people will wait and see what you decide than take the risk to think for themselves with you. You will achieve a greater payoff when people see you as a leader who authentically cares about them more than when you are acting as the organizational fixer.

To trust you enough to work with you inside the Discomfort Zone, people have to feel you believe in them possibly even more than they believe in themselves. They know you are dedicated to seeing them succeed. You sense their hopes and dreams, their desire to grow, and possibly, their yearning to connect to a higher purpose.[7] If the times you help people move closer to their aspirations is what inspires you to come to work and be a leader, you will enjoy working with them in the Discomfort Zone.

To be successful with this stance, you must be willing to develop your capacity for self-observation, including recognizing in the moment or soon after when you have judged and limited a person's growth. Trust is a major component for using the Discomfort Zone successfully. Do ongoing work on recognizing the impact you have on others, especially when you are upset or frustrated. It will also help to increase your willingness to admit your human fallibilities. People feel better when they know their leader or coach makes mistakes, too.

Your Willingness to Seek Out These Opportunities

Many leaders operate with the assumption that if people want something they will ask for it. This belief is not true for many reasons, including cultural views on approaching authority and the negative implication ascribed to asking for help. You will miss opportunities to develop people if you don't reach out to them. Check to see if you believe in any of these myths.

Myth 1
My employees don't want me to ask questions. They just want me to give them answers so they can get back to work.

This is a myth of convenience. If you prefer not to spend the time on development conversations and fear challenging people to think differently, you will tell this story. But people enjoy learning and improving more than they like being dependent on you. According to the research compiled by Daniel Pink, two of the three major motivators of high performance are autonomy and mastery.[8] If you want continuous great results, you need to continuously expand their minds.

Myth 2
If they need something from me or don't understand something, they will ask.

No matter what your title is, people might not feel comfortable letting you know they can't figure something out. They might have a history of other bosses, parents, and teachers belittling them for not knowing everything. People appreciate you asking, "What would be the best thing I could do to support you right now?" If they can't think of anything specifically, offer the gift of your time. A private conversation could reveal an opportunity to expand their thinking.

Myth 3
No one is complaining, so everything is fine.

You may be a good leader but you aren't perfect. Leaders who don't spend time sitting with their people and asking questions about how things are going are out of touch with the challenges their people face. When you keep your fingers on the pulse of your team by asking about their challenges, opinions, and concerns, you will know what they need to maintain motivation.

Myth 4
If a good person does something bad, it won't happen again. They will self-correct.

This is the most common rationalization for avoiding what could be a difficult conversation. Whether you worry that people won't like you or they will react poorly and you won't know what to do, you need to let people know when their actions have had an undesirable outcome. The sooner you share this information, the better. Then if you sense resistance, you can transition the conversation to embrace a coaching approach.

Myth 5
The best employees want to be left alone to do their work.

High achievers want positive feedback. They want recognition for their good work. They want a steady stream of interesting projects with indicators of success. And they want you to challenge their thinking so they can continuously grow. Don't risk losing your best people. Use the Discomfort Zone to grow their minds on a regular basis.

When you trust in people's capabilities for learning and growth, why wouldn't you want to help them rise above their current proficiency? This should be your highest priority as a leader. Look for opportunities for Discomfort Zone conversations as a part of your role as a leader.

Your Purpose for a Conversation in the Discomfort Zone

Before having a Discomfort Zone conversation, explore your reasons for having the conversation and be honest about your expectations. Have you already decided what the acceptable next step will be? You may have a desire to help the person see his work or himself differently, but you can't be attached to how the conversation will progress or what the outcome will be if you want to stay in the zone. If you can't be open to this, you will end up forcing the conversation in the direction you want it to go. This will undermine the purpose of your discussion. Your purpose is to encourage the other person to think for himself, not to tutor, cajole, or influence someone to see your point of view.

Check Your Assumptions

Do you have any preconceived notions about the person that could get in the way of trusting her to find her way even if it takes some time and lessons learned? If you have some limiting assumptions about the person, can you put them aside for the time it takes to test the person's ability to grow? If so, you will be able to allow the conversation to twist and turn on its own, a necessary condition of using the Discomfort Zone. If not, you will limit her growth and possibly damage her confidence, hurting future conversations about her progress.

Choose Your Emotions

When you think about the person and the situation you want to address, do strong emotions arise? Will you be able to release these emotions if they surface during the conversation? Can you accept that the person responds to challenges differently than you do, that his style and speed for processing, learning, and trying out new behaviors are different from yours? Before having a conversation in the Discomfort Zone, envision what could happen, including the worst case scenario. Choose how you want to respond. A clear vision acts as a dress rehearsal that will help you get through the real thing.

As the leader, you set the emotional tone of the conversation. You need to hold a positive emotional intention as well as a developmental purpose throughout the conversation.

You also need to practice patience during the conversation and beyond. The process of sustaining changes in self-perception and behavior could take time. The person you are trying to reach may decide to move forward but then hit a wall of fear and skepticism and fall back. His natural defenses will kick in against the pain of growth. Being there to coach him through the fog of transition is as important as the initial breakthrough conversation.

Be fascinated by the human in front of you. Don't let him frustrate you with his resistance. Don't let him fool you with a false face of ennui. And definitely, don't resort to threatening or bribing him. He needs you to stay calm and intentional throughout the conversation.

Their Levels of Willingness, Desire, and Courage

People don't change because you want them to. They might not even change if they want to. Three conditions must be present for a person to effectively engage with you in this conversation: willingness, desire, and courage. If the person is willing to work with you to see things differently, he believes the conversation has a payoff he desires, and he has the courage to let go of old habits of thinking, there is a good chance the conversation will be both successful and meaningful.

Willingness to Talk

You can't insist someone have an exploratory conversation with you and expect it to be fruitful. You need to declare your intention and then gauge if she is willing to work with you for at least part of the process. If she ever feels forced to participate, willingness will dissipate. She will, instead, become compliant, which blocks new realizations. Let her know she can call an end to the conversation at any time.

To maintain willingness, always acknowledge the person's perspective as valid even if it varies from yours. Never make her feel wrong. If you do not judge her, she may trust you, which is necessary to having a successful conversation. If she trusts you are holding her best interest throughout the conversation, and that you will give her time and space to process the conversation in any way that works for her, she will stay with you even when the tension is thick.

Desire Based on a Personal Value

Unless there is a payoff based on something the other person truly wants, willingness will not endure. There won't be a breakthrough in thinking without some desire for the outcome. You have to consider what this might be before you have the conversation, and then be open to discovering that he might have a different desire that would inspire the change during the conversation. Never assume you know someone too well to ask him what he wants.

Payoffs that inspire change are usually related to something the person values, including being seen as a leader, being respected by peers, mastering skills that make goals easier to reach, earning the chance to be given challenging projects and adventures, carving out more time with family, and gaining more peace of mind. Tying the change to someone's personal values and career dreams will help to ensure long-term results.

The Courage to Look Within

A Discomfort Zone conversation is also a hero's journey.[9] You are taking someone on an adventure of self-exploration where she may need to battle mental habits. The battle takes courage. You need to create a sense of safety before going deep into the conversation, and then maintain this sense of safety even when you challenge her thoughts for her courage to persist.

There will be times when she will refuse to accept the challenge. You can't make people feel courageous. If, however, she trusts your intention is for her to improve based on the potential you see, you should be able to help her move forward when the demons arise. Helping someone muster the courage to say, "Yes!" when she feels awkward, afraid, or unhappy is one of the greatest gifts you can give her.

If you want to make a real difference for someone, I challenge you to step into the Discomfort Zone. It is an amazing process to facilitate. As a side benefit, you will learn more about yourself.

CHAPTER ONE: Key Points to Remember

1. Using the Discomfort Zone is not the same as initiating a typical challenging conversation. It is a method of coaching used when it is clear that a shift in perception or sense of self would be helpful to the person. You don't have a message to deliver; you desire someone to expand her awareness to see her situation and herself in a different light. You don't tell her what you want; you want her to discover, create, or unveil a new reality on her own. In short, you want her to think for herself. You are the facilitator of this process.

2. This book teaches a style of leadership coaching not widely practiced in organizations. It includes how to use challenging questions and reflective statements to help a person confront his rationalizations and see his blind spots, leading to changes in how he sees himself and his world. This style of coaching achieves more profound behavioral changes than other approaches.

3. The specific circumstances needed for this approach to be successful include the right time in the person's development; your belief in the person's potential; your willingness to seek out these conversations; your purpose for the conversation; and the person's levels of willingness, desire, and courage. It is up to you to seek out Discomfort Zone opportunities, especially with your employees who desire to learn and grow.

4. If the person has a baseline of skills and knowledge, you can energize her using *what she knows* instead of exhausting her with *what you know*. You must believe in people and be dedicated to helping them realize their hopes and dreams; their trust in you is built on this.

5. You need to hold a positive emotional intention throughout the conversation. Be patient, be curious, and be open to what transpires.

6. If the person is willing to see things differently, if he believes the conversation will have a payoff he desires, and if he has even a little bit of courage to let go of old habits of thinking, there is a good chance your Discomfort Zone conversation will be both successful and meaningful.

If you are committed to being the best leader you can be, a journey into the Discomfort Zone will help you achieve this noble goal.

Chapter Two

What Comes First

"You can't fake caring."

Len Roberts,
Former Chairman and CEO of
Radio Shack

I had been listening to my client, the CEO of a chemical company, complain for at least five minutes. His employees didn't care, his administrator was incompetent, the economy was a disaster, his customers were idiots, and the traffic was out of control. When I felt I had an opening, I said, "Wah, wah wah."

He said, "Oh my God. I sound like that?"

"Ed, name one thing in our life right now that you are excited about. What is one thing that makes you smile? Better yet, what is one thing that makes you laugh out loud?"

"I'm being an ass, aren't I?" he said.

"I think you aren't aware of who you are being at all, at work or in your life. What are you so angry about?"

After the long pause I'm used to getting from my clients, he declared, "I have no life."

We had never talked about his private life before. I didn't know until that day he had gone through a divorce the year before. When he shared with me what his typical day looked like, he made the revelation that he was putting all of his attention into work to avoid his lonely life. This led to him putting undue pressure on his employees, especially his committed administrator, as he saw them through his lens of negativity. In the end, he agreed it was time to take a vacation. He even promised me he would go dancing, something he had loved doing all of his life before the divorce.

If you thought this seemed too easy, you are right. We had developed a foundation of trust I could count on. This chapter explores how to establish enough trust in a relationship so you don't have people shutting down, walking out, or hanging up on you when you share reflections and ask tough questions. *When they trust your intentions, your direct observations and questions will have the desired impact.*

If you thought my response was rude, you would have been right if I didn't listen to him well enough to have confidence both in what I was sensing and how I would handle his response. I didn't fall into the trap of sympathizing with him. I didn't jump into problem solving the issues he presented. I knew I needed to be firm, even edgy. Then I knew when to use compassion and when to use humor to lighten the mood.

Above all, I deeply respected and cared about the human I was listening to. From this position, I could sense what was needed to break through his barrier.

Your first step is to establish and sustain a bond strong enough to work inside the Discomfort Zone. In the process, the person feels safe enough to express emotions as his or her brain sorts through beliefs and attachments. When the person stays with you even when he feels uncertain, vulnerable, and off balance, learning can occur.

The Doorway to the Discomfort Zone

There is a right way for walking people into the Discomfort Zone. If you try to push people into the zone too quickly, they will feel bullied. Your great questions will drive up their defenses instead of break down their barriers. You have to make sure people trust the conversation will be beneficial for them.

First, ask yourself if you are able to be mentally and emotionally present 100 percent during the conversation. Malcolm Forbes said, "Presence is more than being there." There is always an energetic connection when people come together.[1] Something happens in the space "between brains" when people interact.[2] Your intention for the conversation, your emotions, and your regard for the person will impact their willingness, desire, and courage to change. You have to stay present and aware to sustain trust throughout the conversation.

Once you are present, ensure there is a *safety bubble* that encompasses you and the other person so he will let you inside his head. There are four things you need to do to create the *safety bubble* of trust: settle into the flow, set and maintain your emotional-based intention, hold the highest regard for both yourself and the other person, and trust the process no matter what transpires.

Settle into the Flow

Find a quiet, private place away from your computer and other distractions that could steal your brain away. Clear your mind of worries or pressing obligations. You need to move your attention into the present moment.

During the conversation, your mind won't be blank; your brain will subtly monitor the dynamics of the interaction. If you are calm, comfortable, and present to yourself as well as the other person, you will notice your thoughts, emotions, and the shifts in how your body feels without losing what they are saying and meaning. Being interested in both the person's reactions and your own will help you know what to say to move the conversation forward.

In other words, when you are fully present, you are capable of perceiving what is occurring in yourself as well as in the person you are with. You aren't a neutral observer. You may notice you tense up when she shows resistance so you can choose to feel compassion before you respond. You may notice your urge to fill in the silence when their brain is trying to resolve a mental conflict. So you relax, allowing time for the person to make sense of the new truth formulating in her brain. You may notice your desire to back off or save her by saying, "It's no big deal." Instead, you stay resolute with the process. You sense the changes taking place in both of you when you are fully present.

My presencing routine is to first release any tension I am holding in my body so that I feel relaxed, and then I clear my mind, breathe into my belly, and think the words *I care*. I allow my breath to flow deeply into my body so I feel the words sink into my core. If I am on the phone, I choose to sit in a quiet place away from computer. If I am visiting a client, I make sure we sit far away from these distractions as well. With this setup, I can allow the conversation to spontaneously unfold while I notice what happens within us and between us throughout the process.

The only words I deliberately prepare to say are an opening statement to establish the intention of the conversation, and I close by offering to support whatever was determined as the next step. During the conversation, I do my best to stay open and aware, allowing the conversation to be unconstrained, instinctive, and honest.

This process is similar to what artists and others involved in the creative process experience when they are composing. Neuroscientists at the National Institute on Deafness and Other Communication Disorders took twelve professional rappers and ran them through an fMRI machine.[3] They noticed that although the brain's executive functions were active at the start and end of a song, during freestyle, the parts of the brain responsible for self-monitoring, critiquing, censoring, and editing were deactivated. In this context, the researchers explained that the rappers were "freed from the conventional constraints of supervisory attention and executive control" so sudden insights could easily emerge.

In other words, the rappers switched off their inner critic and analyzer. This allowed for more activity in the inner brain where sensory processing and the eruption of new ideas takes place. Other researchers have found similar reactions when studying what happens when people enter a "state of flow."[4]

In the Discomfort Zone, the art is to apply this flow state of creativity and performance to your conversation. As with the rappers, when you become present, aware, and in flow, unrestrained questions and reflections emerge. Then you skillfully and courageously use what emerges to help people see themselves and their issues differently. You will learn how to better hear what you need to say in the next two chapters.

When in a flow state, you are also better able to maintain composure if tensions rise. You will be challenging how people define their sense of self and the world; they may get defensive as they protect these definitions. Your calm reaction will maintain the integrity of the safety bubble as they work to grasp a new view of reality.

Countless books, articles, and blog posts teach the art of being here now. Find a routine that works for you. While in conversation, if you catch yourself drifting away or your brain is filling with critical thoughts, take a deep breathe into your belly. Let your thoughts flow out as you exhale. Relax your body. Remember why you are there. If you aren't here now, the conversation won't work.

Set and Maintain Your Emotional-Based Intention

Whether you lead a small team or an entire organization, there is inherent judgment built into organizational systems based on hierarchies, performance assessments, and traditional definitions of success. Many people are suspicious when asked to be open and honest. Even if you *create a safety bubble* by refraining from judgment during the conversation, gaining the other person's trust in the genuineness of your intentions could take more than one conversation.

You need to consider both your relationship with the person and the company cultural norm around trust in leadership—the level of trust in the leaders in general—so you know if you need to work on relationship building before you attempt Discomfort Zone conversations. Even if you think people have a general trust in the leaders in your company, personal trust might be low. A recent event could have impacted the person's ability to trust others including you. Don't forget that some people don't trust leaders no matter what!

Never expect trust in your first conversation; go in ready to read the person's level of comfort with you. Then you can assess how much trust you need to build into the interaction and if this process will take a few sessions before the person will open up to you.

If you are to succeed in building trust, a person must feel your intentions are in his best interest throughout the conversation and beyond. Your needs and emotions will impact the conversation even if you have been trained to put on a poker face. As soon as you shift your attention to figuring out how to get what you want regardless of what he wants, trust is impaired if not lost. His brain will shut down instead of open up.

If you are there to help a person think, you must be willing to let his thoughts have a life of their own. You may know what is possible for him and what is stopping him from achieving a brilliant outcome, but never lose sight that the journey belongs to him. You are his thinking partner, not a puppeteer.

The Discomfort Zone process uses inquiry to promote self-discovery instead of instructing people to accept your point of view. People, including teenagers, are more likely to change their minds when they discover something on their own than when they are told what is good for them. Once you are comfortable with the process, using the Discomfort Zone is actually easier to do than trying to get results by sharing your knowledge and wisdom no matter how profound you are. This is especially true when it comes to breaking through hardened beliefs, ego defenses, and habitual behavioral patterns.

Your intention is to use the Discomfort Zone to help people to not only see their walls, but to see how their beliefs, defenses, and patterns are limitations instead of steadfast truth. You are there to help them create the breakthrough they can't do for themselves because you want the best for them, not because you want them to think like you.

Your commitment to them must be evident from the beginning to the end. You've seen how quickly people get defensive when they don't like what they hear. I'm sure you, too, have engaged in a verbal battle after receiving criticism, or have mentally checked out the moment someone offered to give you feedback.

The people you are engaging must know that you are doing this to help them grow, not for your self-interest or organizational goals. They must know you are there because you care for them, you trust them, and you want to serve their higher good, not your own.

Even if a broader goal will be met, the present conversation must have an emotional intention focused on the person you are with. This intention will help the person handle the vulnerability she may feel as the walls start cracking. With a positive intention based on seeing her think more broadly for herself, her discomfort will feel purposeful instead of like an attack.

To do this, you have to remain open and curious to what will unfold. You are listening for thinking patterns to examine together, not answers that match your beliefs. You are curious about her assumptions, inquiring how she knows these thoughts are true, not judging whether they are right or wrong. As she searches for evidence to support her beliefs, you may notice contradictions in her reasoning. From here, you can find the reflections, questions, and moments of silence that help her question her own thinking.

Your openness, caring, and curiosity make it possible for a different truth, belief, or understanding to emerge. Her sense of reality expands.

Most people you encounter want to be free from their mental blocks and struggles. To reveal them to you, however, to allow you to explore their thoughts, feelings, needs, and desires, they have to fully trust you. You have to release your own attitudes, assumptions, and positions to allow the process to unfold.

You also have to allow them to fully tell their story before you start your inquiry. If you try to go too deep too fast, they will not believe in your intention. They will fortify their walls and the conversation will go nowhere.

It's not that as a leader, there won't be times when you have to be more direct with what you want people to do. Those are different conversations. When in Discomfort Zone conversations, however, your purpose is to expand a person's ability to see blind spots, solutions, and possibilities she couldn't see on her own. Inquiry is both your primary tool and your state of mind.

Holding the Highest Regard for Both Yourself and the Other Person

Conversations in the Discomfort Zone require a feeling of respect in addition to trust. Your regard for the person is critical to the outcome. Even if you disagree with his perspective, you have to honor the human in front of you knowing he is doing his best to survive and succeed with what he knows. Hopefully, you can help him realize what else he can know.

According to the classic work of philosopher and teacher, Martin Buber, there are a number of positions you can take with a person that will impact the relationship.[5] The major positions include: *Me and You, I and It, I and Thou*, and *Thou and Thou*. These positions represent how you feel about the person you are with.

These days, especially with all our technological distractions, we enter into too many personal conversations from the position of *Me and You* or *I and It*, in which we don't really see the person before us. Here, you need to shift to the position *I and Thou* or *Thou and Thou* to establish and maintain trust in the interaction. How you hold your regard for the person is as important as the words you choose to say.

Me and You

This first state represents disconnection. When you talk to people quickly between doing other things, you might as well be strangers. There is no connection between you. You say things mindlessly. You may make suggestions, ask for actions, or share your observations, but you don't encourage conversation. You don't even need agreement. You just want acknowledgment you were heard. You aren't aware of your impact because you are disconnected to them. When was the last time someone talked *at you*, oblivious to how you felt about what they were saying? Consider the possibility that you do this to others more than you realize.

I and It

This second state represents separation. When you have a goal to achieve and you want the people you are with to either see your point of view or take a particular action, they are a means to an end for you. You might speak in a caring and respectful manner, but your intention is based on your goals, not theirs. If they disagree with you, you listen for points you can use to better state your case. You might concede on a few points, but you privately judge the person or his ideas as stupid. You are conversing together, but mentally you are separated. If this is a team situation, the position is *Us and Them*.

I and Thou

This third state represents relating. When you fully relate to someone, he will feel you respect his intelligence and capabilities. The word *thou* represents how important you feel he is and how much value you place on your time together. Even if your opinions differ, you trust he is doing his best to figure things out with what he has learned so far in this lifetime. It is easier for someone to trust your intention when he feels you relate to him as *thou*. If you can't reach this state, you may not be able to enter the Discomfort Zone.

Thou and Thou

This fourth state represents unity. Buber's work does not mention this state. In recent decades, however, a conceptual framework that defines the energetic dynamics between two people has been identified in quantum physics and neuroscience. Margaret Wheatley's seminal work, *Leadership and the New Science*, brought the effects of relationship networks into the language of leadership.[6] More recently, the presence of mirror neurons in the brain—which help us sense someone's unspoken intentions and emotion—has been integrated into many corporate communications training programs.[7] If the shifts in your biology and the energy you emanate through your emotions and intentions affect the interaction, then your sense of being a significant partner in the relationship is just as vital as the respect you hold for others.

To create a *Thou and Thou* connection defined by two people who are both intelligent, creative, and important, you have to remove the needs that force you to protect your sense of "I" in your conversation. Specifically, you need to release the needs to be right, to be respected, to be liked, or to be in control.[8] When you feel the urge to explain yourself, let it go. When the other person's resistance feels disrespectful, unless he or she is intentionally causing you harm, don't take it personal and let it go. When you worry he won't like you if you challenge his assumptions and reactions, muster the courage to let it go, and speak up. If you feel the conversation is out of your control, reiterate the outcome you agreed to work on together and ask if it is still valid. Hopefully, you will put the conversation back on track. Once you put these needs aside, you may experience a merging of the minds.

Releasing your "I" is difficult. Start by trying not to get caught up in your web of evaluations and judgments. Your "I" feeds on your opinions and personal needs. When you free up your mind, you can experience the flow state as two whole, actualized people exploring possibilities together.

Releasing Your "I" Exercise

Try walking around for twenty minutes, noticing your world without your "I" getting in the way. See if you can notice things, situations, and people as if you have never seen them before. What would you notice? What colors and details pop out? What events and people make you smile? There is so much we miss when our "I" leads us through life.

In actuality, even with practice, you will probably vacillate between thinking from your "I" state and releasing it as you develop presence and awareness. *Thou and Thou* is an aspirational state. When you feel the urge to defend your point of view or to save the person from feeling any discomfort, remember to relax, exhale, and remind yourself you are there to help the other person think. When you release your "I", the energetic field you create encourages the person to explore with you. It's worth the effort.

Assessing Your Position Exercise

Carry a notepad with you for one day. Every few hours, recall all the interactions you had with people, from store clerks to family to people you work with. Identify which position you held in each exchange:

Me and You (disconnected)

I and It (separated, focused on your goal or desire)

I and Thou (relating, focused on connecting and caring)

Thou and Thou (unity, in a spontaneous flow state)

Also note if the outcome would have improved if you claimed a different position. Set goals for shifting your position in future interactions to get a different result.

Trust the Process

To achieve a meaningful result, you have to trust the value of the Discomfort Zone process even when you aren't sure it is working. Their reactions could be unnerving to both of you. Remember, there is a range of possible reactions when you share a significant reflection or question from a minimal response such as, "Oh, yeah, I see what you mean" to the person gasping with embarrassment and then begging for time to think about what occurred. The person might even get angry when it is difficult to accept the truth.

In other words, it might take a few seconds to construct a new perspective or it could take a few minutes, hours, or days. The person might leave the conversation without a clear direction forward. The dismantling process can take time as the defenses in the person's brain battle with the new truth trying to emerge.

I have had clients scream at me, claiming I have no idea what they are experiencing, only to come back days later telling me how differently they see their situation now. Sometimes they just change their behavior without verbally acknowledging the shift in beliefs. I trust that they will come to a deeper understanding as they experience a change in their results or relationships, and then we can talk about what changed for them.

If you lose trust in the process, you will revert to finding an easy solution that probably won't have much impact over time. You may then reinforce the person's habit of relying on you for answers and not thinking for him- or herself. Or your acquiescence could signal support for the person's deficient or unhealthy behavior. You both lose when you give in.

The three pitfalls to watch out for are: your own discomfort, your anxiety with the other person's discomfort, and your own impatience.

Your Own Discomfort

Your own brain has automatic defense mechanisms that are naturally on alert at all times. When the conversation begins to feel risky, messy, or emotionally unstable, you need to breathe and recall your emotional intention for the conversation.

One of my clients told me she is good at being direct and honest with most people at work, but in her new position, there is one person she shies away from even when there are important issues to resolve. She said this person agrees to have conversations with her but then cancels, saying he has something to do and will get back to her when they have time to talk (which never happens). Instead of confronting this recurring behavior, my client lets it go, leaving the issues unresolved. I asked her, "What are you afraid you will find out if you ask him the real reason he won't meet with you?" She said, "I'm afraid it will become clear he doesn't respect me or my position, and I need his respect right now because everything feels new."

My question led to a deeper conversation around what is true about her fears and what was speculation. She decided to ask her colleague to lunch instead of a formal meeting. She felt they needed to know each other better. This also gave her the opportunity to ask how best to approach him when she had problems to discuss. They agreed on a way they could work better together.

Vincent Van Gogh said, "Let's not forget that the little emotions are the great captains of our lives, and we obey them without realizing it." You need to notice when your body tenses up or your breathing shortens, so you can release the tension and return to being present. If the person isn't ready to explore with you, you might back off and come around to the question later in the conversation or schedule another session to give him time to think.

The person may never be ready to have this conversation with you. That may be the reflection you need to share after repeated attempts. Then if there is a problem that needs to be resolved, share the consequences he might face if he doesn't work on finding a solution with you. Don't threaten him. Just be clear about what won't happen if he doesn't change his point of view. Don't forget your intention for the conversation. You are there to help him think through the situation if he is willing. If he isn't willing, you may choose a different type of conversation to have with him. And don't flip into using more supportive, encouraging, and evasive language just because you don't like how you feel when someone shows resistance.

Your Anxiety with the Other Person's Discomfort

The other person's discomfort is inherent in the process. When you ask a question or share a reflection that represents a conflict with his or her current reality, you affect a person's equilibrium. She can't help but react even if the reaction is slight confusion. It takes time for the brain to form a new meaning based on what she is learning about herself and her reality. If she doesn't try to verbally dance into another subject, there will be an uncomfortable silence. The experience can, but not always, lead to the person feeling embarrassed, sad, or even angry because she has not realized before what she is now able to see. Or she might just feel a bit off-balance.

Your job is to maintain your safety bubble while she is going through whatever emotions she experiences as the new awareness emerges. Remember your intention. Remember your goal of service. Remember you are watching the brain of the person in front of you actually spark, shift, and develop new connections. How awesome is that? Stay alert to the magic that is occurring so you don't get entangled in her reactions.

Your Own Impatience

Finally, the demon you will most have to battle is your own impatience. You will need to be comfortable with allowing for long silences and for letting the process unfold.

When you think you know exactly what is wrong with the other person's thinking, you have to stay with the inquiry process. The moment you think you have to tell him what is wrong with his point of view, you won't know what questions to ask. Your brain will focus in on what you want to say. Then if you slip and tell him what is wrong with his thinking and what he should do next, his brain will shut down. No one likes being made to feel wrong or stupid. He might do what you say, but you haven't developed his mind or helped him feel better about the future.

You also have to be patient with silence. As I mentioned before, silence is often an indication that the reflection or question you asked breached his wall of resistance. Learning is occurring. He will sit almost paralyzed as his brain recombines and reinterprets information, formulating a new way to define the situation. The calm silence you hold allows this creative process to happen.

You've seen this process happen with babies. When you do something that babies have not ever seen before, they stare, often with their mouth open. Eventually, they determine if what they see is funny or scary and they react. Based on what occurs next, they have a new experience to log into their growing mental library.

Adults do the same thing when you ask them a jarring, powerful question. They will often give you *the baby stare*. If the insight doesn't come right away, they might shift their gaze down at the floor or at their hands as their brains work to make sense of what they are learning. When the connections form a new awareness, a person might laugh and say, "Ah, yeah, I'm doing that." She could cry because you have touched a sensitive topic she has avoided. She could be angry with you for pointing out a hole in her thinking. She may be embarrassed when she realizes she's been doing something silly for years and years and years.

When you allow this process to play out, there is power in the moment. The best thing you can do is be patient and allow the person's brain to work.

Discomfort Zone conversations start with ensuring there is a sense of trust, safety, and respect, so when you move into challenging a person's thinking, you and the other person will stay with the process in hopes that a breakthrough will occur. In the process, you hold the space of trust and regard when the person expresses emotions. You know how to release your own discomfort and impatience while the person's brain is sorting through beliefs and attachments. When these conversations become part of your leadership style, you are creating a true learning environment that supports change and personal growth.

CHAPTER TWO: Key Points to Remember

1. To use the Discomfort Zone, you have to first create a safety bubble in which people trust you enough to let you inside their heads.

2. There are four things you need to do to create the safety bubble of trust: settle into the flow, set and maintain your emotional-based intention, hold the highest regard for both yourself and the other person, and trust the process no matter what transpires.

3. Presence allows you to have an awareness of what is occurring in yourself, in the person you are with, and in the space between you.

4. If you are to succeed in building trust, a person must feel your intentions are in his or her best interest throughout the conversation and beyond. Your purpose is to reveal a greater self to the person, not fix his problems or make him into being someone else.

5. If you are truly there to help a person think, you must let her thoughts have a mind of their own. Remain open and curious to what will unfold.

6. Conversations in the Discomfort Zone require you feel respect for the human in front of you. You must hold a position of *I and Thou* or *Thou and Thou* for deeper understanding and mental shifts to take place.

7. To achieve a meaningful result, you have to trust the value of the Discomfort Zone process even when you aren't sure it is working. If you lose trust in the process and either back off or revert to telling a person what to do, you could hurt future attempts to use the Discomfort Zone. Three pitfalls to

watch out for are your own discomfort, your anxiety with the other person's discomfort, and your own impatience.

8. Honor a person's silence with your own. The mind is at work.

Chapter Three

The Map and the Milestones for Your Conversation

"The truth is obtained like gold, not by letting it grow bigger, but by washing off from it everything that isn't gold."

Leo Tolstoy, from *Tolstoy's Diaries*

One of the coaching questions I often ask is: *"How do you know that to be true?"* The answer is always based on personal perception and not absolute laws of the universe, if there are any. Individuals build their own models of reality from whatever bits and bytes are stored in their minds. Even "true facts" relating to the physical world have been up for hot debate in the past century.

Although hundreds of models and theories from philosophy, biology, and psychology seek to explain how humans know things, they all support the fact that social reality is subjective. Plato had it right 2,400 years ago when, in his dialogue *Theaetetus*, he defined *knowledge* as "justified true beliefs." In other words, we make up what we believe to be true based on our education, past experiences, and our hopes for what will transpire in the future.

The beauty of having a subjective sense of reality is that points of view can expand and change. That is the intention of using the Discomfort Zone: to reveal, expand, and alter what is thought to be true.

This doesn't mean you can easily convince people to take on your point of view. In fact, because you have a different view of reality than the people you work with, you may never get their views to match up perfectly with yours. By now I hope you understand that is not the point of this work. Remember your intention is to reveal, expand, and alter what the other person believes is true for her growth and development.

Instead of trying to define reality for her, you are hoping to surprise her speedy brain, ask questions that dissect her mental constructs, and provide reflections that crack the "truths" held in place by her stale rationalizations. This is how you help her think more deeply for herself. In the end, she will respect you more for the questions you asked than your unbound willingness to share your knowledge.

This chapter describes a process for courageously coaching in the Discomfort Zone so people are able to expand their views around what is true and possible. It is not a problem-solving process focused on brainstorming solutions for difficult situations; it is an awareness-expanding process focused on perceiving a situation differently so that a more sustainable solution or beneficial understanding emerges.

How to DREAM Together

In the last chapter, I referred to research that located which regions of the brain were active and which were dormant in the conscious creative state of rappers. Although the rappers consciously prepared the opening and closing words of their music, their censoring and correcting regions went quiet during the middle of the composition, allowing images, ideas, and sensations to freely flow into their conscious awareness, much like what happens when we dream. The aim is to create a similar process when using the Discomfort Zone to coach.

In the DREAM process, you will begin and end the conversation deliberately. At the start, you help the person determine what would be the most beneficial outcome to achieve as a result of the conversation. This could take time to formulate as you help him clarify his view of the problem. At the end of the conversation, the person determines what he plans to do next.

During the conversation, you will reflect and explore what underlies the person's words, beliefs, feelings, desires, and fears until a new view of the situation emerges and it feels like progress has been made. You will not follow linear steps. You may not end with a solid action plan, but it's clear the person is using a new awareness or perspective to assess the situation.

The acronym DREAM stands for these activities:[1]

D = Determine what the person wants as a desired outcome of the conversation

R = Reflect on the experiences, beliefs, and emotions expressed

E = Explore possible sources of blind spots and resistance

A = Acknowledge the emerging awareness

M = Make sure there is a plan or commitment for what is next

The flow should feel spontaneous, not contrived, especially when you dive below the surface and use the unstructured, non-linear steps of reflecting, exploring, and acknowledging. Progress is spurred by the questions you ask and the reflections you share.

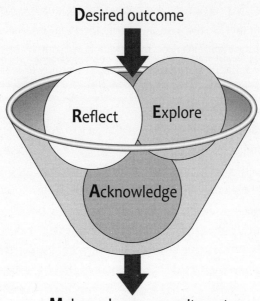

Desired outcome

Reflect **E**xplore

Acknowledge

Make a plan or commitment

In the next chapter, you will learn how to listen in ways that will help you determine what to ask and share as you explore, challenge, and modify the ingredients of their justified true beliefs.

D = Determine what the person wants as a desired outcome of the conversation

When starting a recent coaching conversation, the person said her goal was to work with two of the leaders on her project team to create a solid action plan everyone would agree to. As she started sorting through the possible actions she could take to create the plan, I felt myself losing interest. I could help her explore the best options, but I believed she could do this just as well on her own. I said, "You seem to have solid options to present to your team. What is the real difficulty you need to sort out to get the result you want?"

She hesitated before she said, "I just want them to get their act together and agree to something. Those two guys are on opposite ends of the spectrum on what we need to do, but neither of them is budging. Time is running out. Jobs are on the line. How do I make them see that?"

Her agitation was palpable. I asked, "How responsible are you for the outcome of the project?"

"My job could be on the line, too, but they don't report to me so I can't make them do anything. What if they ignore me?"

"I sense you feel their conflict is ridiculous in light of the urgency of having a plan, so you have a tough message to give but you are afraid they will disagree, or worse, discount you."

"Yes, but I really don't know how they will respond to me."

"If you aren't direct with them, what are the possible outcomes?"

"Something has to happen now or I believe all of our jobs are on the line."

"So I hear your goal is to first figure out how you can overcome your fear around confronting this situation head-on. Right? Then we can explore how you might get them to work together to create a plan they can agree on."

"Actually, I think I know what I want them to do. I just need to say it." Her resolve was much stronger than when we started. The conversation moved toward achieving the newly defined outcome of overcoming her fear so she could confidently present her solution.

Sometimes a new solution is found when figuring out what the person really wants. For example, some people will come to the conversation with a goal to make a decision, but the real problem is that they have made a decision they don't want to admit to. This often happens when someone wants to leave a job or turn down a project but guilt is halting progress. The outcome the person wants to achieve is not to make a decision but to act on the desired option. You discover this when you work to clarify the desired outcome. Another example is when a person says her goal is to stop feeling overwhelmed when she is actually upset over the direction of her career. If you accept the initial goal as the outcome, you will focus on time management. Instead, she may need your help visioning her future. If you dig deeper to find out what she really wants, what she is afraid might happen if she makes certain choices, what is missing for her personally, or what unmet need is triggering her negative emotions, not only will the flow of the conversation be more meaningful but the solution might become crystal clear without much exploration.

People are often unsure about what they really want or they are afraid to speak it out loud. Your job is to help them discover, clarify, and declare what they want. Once their real desires are articulated, the actions they must take are easier to declare and commit to.

It's possible the person does not have a particular outcome in mind when you begin the conversation. He may have only a topic to discuss, such as what to do at business meetings or how to build relationships with peers. You may still need to prod him for at least a preliminary outcome of the conversation, asking questions such as *"What will you find easier to do once we explore this topic?"* or *"What is the issue that is prompting you to talk about this now?"* Do not just ask "What would you like to talk about today?" and leave it at that. The general question may open the conversation but does not ensure a clear and significant outcome.

The person might need to give you some backstory to explain why he wants to discuss something with you, especially if his problem is emotionally taxing. Listen for emotional trigger points, share what you are noticing, and ask how this relates to his present dilemmas to keep him from getting lost in her story.

You might need some perspective to understand what is stopping him from getting what he wants today, but shift the conversation back to clarifying what he really desires as an outcome as soon as the patterns become clear.

Finally, you may go down one path while coaching a person thinking the outcome is clear, but as you begin the exploration, she might quickly come up with a half-baked solution to avoid a deeper conversation. Stop the action if you experience a quick shift from "not knowing what to do" to "I get it; let's move on." Share what you think is happening. Ask *"Do you honestly believe your plan will solve your problem and achieve your outcome once and for all?"* If there are times the solution won't work, she might be willing to further explore what is really at the source of the problem. A new desired outcome could emerge.

Fish for what each person really needs in order to solve the presenting problem. It will help both of you move forward.

R = Reflect on the experiences, beliefs, and emotions expressed

Have you ever argued with someone, possibly your spouse or partner, about something that occurred in the past? This is generally a waste of time. Whether the past is yesterday or years ago, you are likely to disagree over details of the event. Few people have photographic memories, meaning their memory may be phenomenal (but not perfect). The rest of us piece together pictures and data into a story that makes sense to us but rarely matches the recollections of others even if we were together when the event occurred.

The story you tell about a past event is never the absolute truth because, for many biological reasons, you remember only a fraction of what you experience. So when you recall the event, you are making up what you think the details should be. Throw your upbringing, experiences, values, beliefs, assumptions, biases, fears, and desires into the mix, and your story is always your unique version of what happened. To top it off, because you learn new things daily, every time you recall an event it changes.

Yet we live out our lives based on our stories as if they were static and accurate. All of your stories paint the landscape you believe to be reality or *the world according to me*. Jonathan Gottschall, author of *The Storytelling Animal*, says, "Story is so omnipresent that we are hardly aware of how it shapes our lives."[2] You navigate your complex social society based on the stories you recall. This is how you survive.

This means that you and I both have our own map of the world that helps us navigate life. I can't make you believe my map is more real than yours. Nor can you make me or anyone else believe your map is more correct.

You can, however, ask questions that could prompt someone to enlarge and change his or her map. This bigger map will include new ideas if connections are easy to make. If you use reflection and inquiry to uncover inconsistencies, dangers, and opportunities that don't fit with a person's current map, he will change some of the details so his stories make sense again.

The first step requires you hear the person's story about a situation. You have to fully digest his perspective. You aren't just listening to his words; when you listen beyond his words, his stories reveal:

What he feels is most important,

What is causing his frustration, fear, or embarrassment,

What assumptions and beliefs have skewed or limited his perception, and

What he honestly wants to happen regardless of probability or correctness.

You want to prompt to hear his reasoning and ask questions to clarify his beliefs so you both see these ingredients as well as how they impact his story.

An Example Using Reflection

I was working with the vice president of a division being sold to another company. She asked to use the session to determine the direction for her next conversation with one of her managers who was not meeting deadlines for reports important to the transition process. Peers reported that the manager was also very negative in meetings. My client detailed everything she had done so far to help her manager figure out why she wasn't doing the reports, why she was abrasive with her peers, and what she needed to do to get on board with the transition process. The manager was full of excuses but made few attempts to change. My client said she thought the manager was covering up the fact that she didn't have the skills to do her job. The transition was bringing these gaps to light. I asked my client, "What haven't you done to remedy this?"

She paused, sighed, and said, "I haven't done what I should do, let her go."

"What damage will that cause?" I asked.

"Honestly, the new owners want to see if I can make tough decisions. And they want me to bring over only the right team."

"Then there is no damage."

"Shouldn't I be able to turn this around? Aren't I a bad leader for losing one of my people in the process? What's worse, she and I used to be friends. Not now, of course."

"But you said you would be seen as a good leader if you let her go. What is the real loss to you if you make this decision?"

"How about the image of myself being perfect? Or my tendency to think of my team as my friends?"

"Either one sounds good. Pick it and we will work on that today." We ended up with a powerful session in which she redefined her role and definition of *leadership*. She acted on her tough decision that week.

Remember to resist judging the story based on your own story. You have to be open to the other person's interpretation no matter how off the mark you think she is. The person needs to feel you have respectfully heard her before she will let you poke holes in her story.

To ensure she feels heard, use the reflective techniques such as *summarizing, paraphrasing,* and *asking clarifying questions* that encourage her to share more details so you can fully understand her point of view. This ensures both of you are clear on how she sees her story. Sometimes just helping someone gain clarity about her own thoughts helps her see what else is possible. Summarizing and paraphrasing also helps you keep the conversation on track, especially when you have ramblers who tend to get lost in their backstory.

Be sure to affirm the person's efforts and intentions as you seek to discover his or her perspective. When you sincerely tell someone, *"I know you are trying to be the best leader you can be"* or *"I can tell you are committed to getting a good result on this project"* you encourage disclosure. Most people are doing their best with what they think they know. Tell them you know this. This shows you understand their good intentions. They will be more open to exploring what else there is to know.

Another powerful reflection tool is called *mirroring*. By repeating back to the person the key ideas and opinions he stated using his words and identifying his current emotions, you are literally holding up a verbal mirror in which he can witness how his thought and emotional processes are working. When you mirror their words, people observe how they assign meaning to events. They catch the judgments they are making about people. They see how they are rationalizing their decisions or inability to decide.

When mirroring, make sure your tone is encouraging and inquisitive, not threatening. You aren't throwing anything back into his face. You are thoughtfully giving him the chance to see and hear himself from the outside in. Your sentences will start with words such as *"So I heard you say you think the reasons this is happening are . . ."* or *"You got very angry (excited, quiet, defensive, etc.) when you said . . ."* Do not add your interpretations about what he said or expressed. Keep your opinions, judgments, and analysis out of the mirror.

Mirroring gives the brain a chance to question itself. You are the brain tickler he needs to see more broadly. If all he needed was to shift his perspective after examining his thoughts, reactions, and behavior, you might not need to further probe his motivations.

One final note about reflecting: in addition to curbing your tendency to judge his version of the story, you need to stay away from leading him to your point of view or suggestions. Your questions will begin with the words "who, what, how, and when" and not, "Did you think about doing . . . ," "Have you tried . . . ," or "Why did you or didn't you do . . ." Remember, you are relaxed, present, and curious about *Thou's* story, not waiting to insert your viewpoints or solutions.

E = Explore possible sources of blind spots and resistance

Once you are both clear on the desired outcome and the person's story around what is keeping her from achieving this outcome, it's time to explore the elements that shaped the story. This exploration is intended to do one or more of the following:

Discern knowns from speculation in his interpretation of events and actions.

Reveal the myths behind his assumptions.

Shine a light on unmet expectations or personal needs that triggered emotions.

Break down barriers that protect a familiar though stifling sense of self and reality.

Uncover possibilities buried under envy, regrets, disappointments, or fear.

You may stir up emotions in your inquiry. If you have created a safety bubble and your intention to serve is clear, the clouds will pass and the view will be much broader.

In this section, you will read examples of what might occur and what types of questions you might ask. This is an organic process. You cannot memorize questions from a list and guarantee they will have the impact you expect. *Formulate your questions based on what the other person tells you, what you sense he or she is leaving out, and what you sense is triggering his emotions and driving his behavior.* Your senses can be wrong; your questions will help him understand himself regardless.

In essence, after the full story is out on the table, explore the beliefs, assumptions, desires, and fears that formulated his point of view. Help him articulate what he would love to do if his brain wasn't editing his words. His blind spots could be truly hidden, and he may be shocked when he first sees them. Or his blind spots may be slightly covered in a way in which you can easily pull off the sheet. Then he may feel silly, irritated, or even sad that he hadn't noticed something so obvious before.

You don't need to know why his brain focuses on or interprets a situation in a particular way; in fact, questions that start with *why* are usually seen as threats and trigger defensiveness. It's better to ask questions such as *"How do you know that to be true?"* or *"What do you know to be absolutely true as opposed to what you fear might happen?"* or *"What is truly stopping you from taking the next step?"* You are looking for him to recognize the beliefs and biases that are shaping his story in the moment.

An Example Exploring Truth

The retiring director of a government agency asked me to coach his executive team to see if I could help them better cope with the transition to a new leader. The first thing I did when I met with the team was to ask each of them to tell me what was going on for them. One by one, each person told me how horrible the situation was. There was no way the board would appoint a new leader as good as the current one. One person was going to retire. Another one was putting all projects on hold. A third hinted he might look elsewhere for work. The rest had similar stories. When they were done, I said, "I hear you feel a great loss with the director leaving. I hear you are afraid of what will happen with a new leader. I hear that you feel helpless because you aren't involved in the decision. This is all understandable. You liked your director very much. You don't expect the board to make a good decision. I get it. But let me ask you, out of all that you shared with me, what do you know to be absolutely true in this moment?"

The Map and the Milestones for Your Conversation

They all gave me *the baby stare* until one man said, "I guess all we really know is that John is leaving."

"Okay," I said. "It is unfortunate you don't know what will happen next. But based on what you know to be true, what do you think you need to do either for yourself or the agency?"

The head of human resources said, "I think we should shore up our succession planning so we can weather any leader." The team enthusiastically agreed. We had a new goal to work on.

Questions that start with *what* are good for exploring. Notice how these questions might deepen the dialogue: *"What is at stake for you?" "What do you believe is making people act this way?" "What did you expect to happen that didn't?" "What do you need to happen to make this okay for you?" "What do you truly believe is possible?" "What will never happen?"*

The words *Are you* can also be used to discern which way the person is leaning on a decision. Although these words lead to a closed question that might get just a yes or no answer, they can also determine what the person has already decided but is not yet willing to admit to or act on. Direct questions such as *"Are you willing to face this challenge head on?" "Are you able to live with the backlash if you know in your heart you are doing the right thing?"* and *"Are you willing to forgive yourself for not being perfect so you can figure out what to do next?"* should lead to a concrete plan of doing or not doing something instead of being paralyzed by indecision.

An Example Exploring Fear

The owner of a big printing shop had been preparing to sell his company for months. When he came close to the date to put out the offer, he kept coming up with dramas at work he needed to fix. He asked to reschedule our session. I asked for five minutes of his time. First, I reflected to him what I saw happening in the past month. Then I said, "No one says you have to sell. You can decide not to if you want. If I put both options on the table, sell or not sell, which choice, if you had made it this morning, leaves you feeling badly?" He said the thought of selling made him sad. I asked, "What's the loss you are afraid of?" He said his colleagues were like family and he didn't like the idea of leaving them behind. "Are you willing to live with the loss?" He said he didn't want to, but he felt telling people he wasn't going to sell after all would be embarrassing. "Which is worse, having people think you are wishy-washy about your big decision or not seeing your work family every day?" He thanked me for helping him decide to stay.

Some points of view are based on personal characteristics, such as whether the person is careful or a risk taker, extraverted or introverted. Be sure not to judge another person's map of the world. Just observe it and explore it with her to see what possibilities she may have missed.

Remember, you aren't there to fix her, convince her, or make her wrong. Do not slip into evaluating what *should be* true and real.

You might also use a direct statement about what you observe before you ask a question to jostle her mind. What are you sensing is the true source of her emotion? Tell her what you sense and ask if it is true. What contradiction did you hear between what she wants and what she isn't willing to do? Share what you heard and allow her response. What decision is it clear she has made but won't admit to? Tell her what you think she has already decided and then let her tell you if this is true or not. What is she afraid to give up or lose if she were bold enough to let go? State what you think she is holding onto and let her tell you if you are right or wrong before you ask what it will take to move forward.

When you are exploring, you are challenging her thinking, not supporting it. You still feel compassion, your intention is still to help her grow and develop, and you want her to find more satisfaction with her decisions in the end. Your emotions and intentions hold the space for people to accept instead of resist the challenge.

As you may have already realized, exploring requires you have courage, both to make the challenge and to accept being wrong even when you believe your assertion is right. If you stay true to your intention and do not try to coerce or lead the person to an answer you want to hear, all your observations and questions are useful in the exploration process. As was explained in Chapter Two, you have to trust the process and allow the awareness to unfold at its own pace.

A = Acknowledge the emerging awareness

This step may feel redundant and simple. It is redundant and simple by design. The intention is for the person to clearly articulate what she now knows to be true to anchor the insight. If you allow her to say, "Okay, I get it now" or some other vague statement, you won't know for sure what she now understands but could easily forget.

Have her clearly articulate what she has learned or what she now understands as a result of the conversation. You can ask questions such as *"What is most important about our conversation that you want to remember?"* or *"Can you state what you discovered in one sentence?"* The act of verbalizing the discovery solidifies the new awareness. It also continues the process of crystalizing the new perspective that could still be changing before your eyes.

This is an important step to take before intentions are declared, goals are set, and promises are made. This is the launching pad for what comes next. When you encourage a person to clearly acknowledge what she has learned, you help her firm up the new foundation she will be walking on going forward.

M = Make sure there is a plan or commitment for what is next

The final piece of the process ensures there is a resolution to the conversation whether the person wanted to define a specific next step or simply wanted clarity on an issue. If the desired outcome was to make a decision or determine what action to take, the closing statement will include tangible actions. When you have a conversation focused on gaining a new perspective, the person might not delineate an action plan at the end of the conversation. The actual shifts in behavior may not become clear until after the person witnesses the situation real time through the lens of his new perspective. The conversation about goals and actions plans might come later, if at all. In this case, you still want to get a commitment about what comes next, even if it is to think more about the issue and speak with you or someone else at a later date.

The measure of a successful Discomfort Zone conversation is based on the achievement of what the other person determined would be the most useful outcome of the conversation. This is the outcome he settled on after discussing his blocks and desires around the situation. Ask if the outcome was achieved and what he feels comes next. If he wanted help making a decision, ask if he is clear about the choice he has made and what steps he will now take. If he just needed to talk through a situation to see it more clearly or to decrease his frustration or fear, ask how he now sees the situation and what he will do based on this new perspective.

Remember that it could take a bit of digging to determine what the person truly wants as an outcome at the beginning of the conversation. Generally, the outcome is to remove the block or interference to achieving what he really wants. When you discover what he really wants to happen, you can work toward removing the barriers stopping him from moving forward. Then wrap up the conversation by having him declare (don't do this for him) if the outcome was achieved, what the plan is if there is one or what he can commit to now, and helping him identify any support he might call on as he moves forward.

For example, the woman earlier in this chapter leading the project team realized that the most critical outcome she wanted to achieve was to overcome her fear for addressing the two leaders in conflict. She didn't need to explore what the project action plan should look like. Instead, she committed to confronting the two leaders with her observation and offering to set up a meeting in which she would mediate their negotiation for a solution.

When we moved into the final piece of the DREAM process, I asked her two questions to ensure she was committed to achieving her desired outcome. I first asked, "How do you feel now about approaching these two leaders?" She said she felt good about the solution and wasn't afraid anymore. I then asked, *"When will you do this?"* I asked this question to make sure she was ready to commit to taking action. She quickly responded, "Monday, of course." I ended the session asking if there was anything else I could do to support her and if she would like the opportunity to check in with me after she met with the leaders.

Notice that I didn't just ask her if she knew what to do and leave it at that. This closed question will get a "yes" answer ranging in tone anywhere from feeble to convincing. Instead, ask questions such as *"Can you tell me what you have decided or determined what you will do next?"* If the person's conviction is not solid, there might be something else you need to discuss. If so, share your reflection and repeat the DREAM process if you found a new crack in the foundation.

A common mistake leaders make is to recap the steps the person is going to take instead of letting the person do it. Don't slip and take his power away after he has done such good work. Let him tell you again what he has learned and what he will do now as a part of wrapping up the conversation. Don't do it for him.

Also, having him declare his next step even if it is only to think more about the issue will boost his courage and hope. He will gain a stronger sense of moving forward.

To put closure on the conversation, end by asking if he needs further support and how he would like to follow up with you. It takes time for people to fully shift the way they see themselves and the world. They may have a new awareness with you, but they may need to see how this thinking plays out in real life. They might need ongoing support. If you can't provide it, see if you can help them determine what they will do to get the support they need to be successful over time.

Final Note: *Remember that having a DREAM conversation is not a linear problem-solving event; it's an organic process that may lead to a brain-popping moment when new definitions of self and reality come to light. Use the techniques from Chapter Seven to sustain your presence and to keep trusting the process.*

CHAPTER THREE: Key Points to Remember

1. We make up what we believe to be true about our social world.

2. A surprising fact, a disruptive question, or a reflection of the gaps in our reasoning can alter how we see ourselves and the world.

3. The DREAM process works to help people see their problems and possibilities from a new and broader perspective.

     D = Determine the desired outcome

     R = Reflect on the experiences, beliefs, and emotions expressed

     E = Explore possible sources of blind spots and resistance

     A = Acknowledge the emerging awareness

     M = Make sure there is a plan or commitment for what is next

4. Spend time clarifying what the person really wants to happen. The desired outcome isn't always clear up front. Often, the more powerful outcome is declared after discovering a person's needs and desires around the situation.

5. Reflecting helps people witness their own thoughts at work when creating their stories. You can summarize, paraphrase, clarify, affirm, and mirror their words and emotions to create this effect.

6. After the full story is on the table, explore how people know what they know so they can observe and assess the beliefs, desires, fears, and assumptions that formulated their point of view. Emotions expressed in the conversation are signs that the blind spots are coming to light and the walls holding

in their perspective are cracking. You have entered the Discomfort Zone. Shifts are taking place.

7. When the person's view of reality makes a distinct shift, have the person articulate what he or she now believes to be true.

8. The measure of a successful Discomfort Zone conversation is based on the achievement of what the other person determined would be the most useful outcome of the conversation.

9. Before concluding, be sure to ask the person to declare what he will do now that the outcome of the conversation was met. Make sure he has a plan or commitment for what is next. End by offering support and determining if follow-up would be helpful.

Chapter Four

How to Listen for What to Say

"It has long been an axiom of mine that the little things are infinitely the most important."

Sherlock Holmes in *A Case of Identity*

Because intuition is often perceived as unexplainable magic or unreliable hooey, it is left out of the list of essential leadership skills. I've seen explanations for intuitive insights ranging from messages from spirits, to a sixth sense available to psychics and wizards, or an evolutionary advantage women have over men. I don't know of any research that confirms these characterizations, including the existence of a woman's intuition though evidence suggests women have learned to heed their inner voice more than men for socially acceptable reasons.

On the other hand, Daniel Kahneman's international bestseller, *Thinking Fast and Slow*, provides a great deal of proof that everyone, even the most concrete thinkers, relies on intuition to navigate daily life.[1] Kahneman demonstrates repeatedly that we make few decisions without a dose of intuition injected into the mix no matter how logical and evidence-based you think you are. Some of our greatest minds, including Albert Einstein, praised intuition as a significant element of good decision making provided it is balanced with data. Intuition is the hallmark quality of the legendary demystifier Sherlock Holmes.

Although he rested his cases on facts, Sherlock Holmes clearly saw both logic and intuition as equal partners in discovering the elements that solved his mysteries. He relied on what Kahneman calls System 1 thinking, which is rapid, instinctive, and emotionally based. He was keen at spotting the smallest of details and understood their significance before the meaning could be tested. He is quoted as admonishing Watson for not taking in all that is available to perceive: "You see, but you do not observe. The distinction is clear."[2]

When seeking to discover what else could be true and possible in the Discomfort Zone, you need to be aware of so much more than what you normally see and hear in a casual conversation. Then you test out what you notice through reflections and questions.

To activate your full sensory capabilities, you need to use emotions and visualization to open all the centers in your neural network where you receive input: the brain, the heart, and the gut. Although you might think your logical brain knows best, most human beings have experienced making decisions on *a gut feeling* or *from the heart* and found the outcome to be fulfilling and even lifesaving. Using these centers to perceive a person's emotional state, the level of commitment to a goal, and the person's sources of hesitation will not only help you deduce like Sherlock but also to know what questions to ask to help the person see these things for him- or herself. I believe this is what *using your intuition* means.

There is a growing body of literature that looks at the power of harnessing and aligning the innate intelligences of the head, heart, and gut. For leaders, this alignment leads to greater authenticity as well as effective decision making. In complex business environments—when under pressure and swift thinking is needed—the leaders who operate from their guts and hearts as well as their heads are more adaptable and successful.[3]

The inspiration for many researchers, teachers, and leaders to look at the power of listening to your gut is based on Dr. Michael Gershon's book, *The Second Brain*.[4] Gershon documents how the vast network of neurotransmitters found in the gut learn, store memories, and process input in similar operations to the brain found in your head. According to Dr. Gershon, the gut brain has 100 million neurons and uses every class of neurotransmitter found in the brain to process input you receive.

Prior to Gershon's work, Dr. Andrew Armour explored how the neural network in the heart learns, remembers, feels, and senses. Dr. Armour coined the term *heart brain*.[5]

The head brain has language so we listen to it, but the signals sent from your heart and gut provide you with critical data you can use to fully comprehend what is going on in the complex human you are conversing with. There is so much more he is saying to you beyond the words coming out of his mouth. You need to access your head and heart to hear.

Listening to Your Three Centers when You Are Alone

It is good practice to first recognize the different information each center provides when you have a decision to make. Researchers Grant Soosalu and Marvin Oka identified three core functions for these three processing centers.[6] Your *head brain* reasons, analyzes, synthesizes, and makes meaning of what is perceived. Your *heart brain* activates based on how the presenting situation relates to your aspirations and desires, ranging on the scale from responding to the joy of achieving what you most desire to sensing that what you hoped for is out of reach. Your *gut brain* reacts to impulses of self-preservation, including reactions based on fear and the impulse or will to act based on courage.

Scientifically, these divisions are simplified because impulses in the neural network are constantly interacting; all parts of the nervous system overlap, making it hard to clearly define what controls our thoughts and actions. Practically, they make sense. Notice the different sensations in the following circumstances. What happens when you think you need to understand something better before you can make a decision? Do you feel anxious? Do your thoughts start racing? What happens when you are excited about your new idea because it is going to make a big positive difference in the results? Does your heart beat faster? Is it hard to stop smiling? What happens in your body when you are angry about the new policy because no one asked you about the extra work you will now have to do? Does your stomach tighten? Do you have an urge to pace, throw your arms around when speaking, or hug your body or clasp your hands when you can't express what you feel? Your body is trying to talk to you.

Self-Assessment—Awareness of Three Intelligences

Say the following sentences out loud. Speak the words as if you are truly feeling them. Wait at least two seconds between each statement. As you speak, notice the part of your body that either opens or tenses up with each statement:

"You don't understand. I need to read the entire proposal before I give my answer."

"Okay, I now understand the situation completely."

"I really love it when I am able to spend hours doing that."

"I appreciate what you did for me."

> "I shared my idea with you in confidence and then you told everyone. I don't feel I can trust you now."

> "I am so mad I could scream! I am not going to take this anymore."

> "I'm going ahead with the project no matter what anyone says."

> "No, wait. I'm afraid we will lose everything we have worked so hard for if that happens."

If you didn't feel any difference in your body, it could mean you are out of practice connecting with your emotions so your head brain dominates right now. To strengthen your ability to listen to yourself more deeply, set aside time each week to practice moving your awareness into the three centers of your body. Choose a decision you have to make. It can be as small as deciding when to schedule a phone call you have been putting off or as large as making a decision that will affect your career. The following exercise will help you reconnect with your body beyond your brain so you can better understand your emotional reactions and make better decisions for yourself.

Practice Exercise—Using Your Head, Heart, and Gut

1. Consider a decision you need to make. Be curious. Think about the facts. Consider the pros and cons. What points come to the forefront?

2. Pause, clear your mind, and take a breath. Think of someone you care about or something you love to do. Smile and feel your heart as it beats with your breath. Say the word love or gratitude or choose another word that opens your heart. Now consider the same big decision

you need to make, keeping your awareness around your heart. What points come to the forefront? How do these points differ from what emerged when you considered the decision using only your head? Notice how the points relate more to your desires than to the facts and details.

3. Make sure you are sitting up straight and not hunched over reading this book. Take a deeper breath into your belly. Recall a time you felt gutsy and determined in spite of your fear. Remember the moment you moved forward, when you jumped up, ran to the cliff, took the leap, or spoke your mind. As you inhale, say and feel the word courage. Let the word settle into the core of your body as you exhale. Consider your decision one more time. What points come to the forefront? How do these points differ from what arose when you were thinking through your head and heart? Did you sense any fear, loss, or regret? Did you feel a sense of urgency or impetus to move forward? Maybe you recognized a real and valid reason for saying no or yes that wasn't clear before. How does thinking through your gut impact your decision?

Before you make your decision, balance all the points that arose in all three steps of this exercise to confidently make the best choice with what you now know. Practice this exercise as often as you can to create the habit of listening to all three of your processing centers.

Three-Centered Listening to Others

As I have said more than once, it is not good practice to memorize questions and use them as a formulaic technique. When you are trying to remember a good question you used before, you aren't fully listening to the person you are with. You are more likely to frustrate people than encourage them to think.

The question that is likely to disrupt someone's thinking patterns and break through the wall protecting his or her view of reality will come directly out of the interaction. You must be present and aware of what's happening to know what to say. Then you can formulate questions based on what you are noticing when you have a gut, heart, or cognitive reaction.

You will probably need to break the habit of listening only from your head. When you use only your head to hear, you tend to move the conversation quickly toward goals, missing the nuances that provide clues to the real root of the problem. The process is mechanical and delivers incremental change at best.

You see this oversight play out daily. Leaders define corporate missions based on market needs or revenue goals (head) instead of discovering what will inspire their employees to give their best effort (heart). Team members argue about the budget, task assignments, and accountability (head) instead of asking one another about what matters most to them about a project, what each person hopes to contribute, and what they are afraid could happen if circumstances don't play out a certain way (heart and gut). When we listen to one another from all three centers, conflicts are more quickly resolved and people feel more motivated to act.

When you listen to someone with your body, the results can lead to a breakthrough moment because you are receiving so much more information to consider. You slow down the conversation by trusting that if a solution is needed, it will come from the person out of the broader awareness he or she will have. Then use firm compassion to bring attention to the subtle hints and to inquire about what is difficult to face. Although the conversation can be uncomfortable for both of you, the new awareness provides a different perspective on a difficult situation and often, a renewed sense of hope.

Recent studies demonstrate the legitimacy of listening with more than your head brain. A team of researchers led by Marc-André Reinhard of the University of Manheim in Germany found that unconscious thinking gives people a chance to integrate the rich, complex information needed for accurate lie detection.[7] The team found that the participants who were kept from consciously analyzing if a person was lying or not had more accurate results than those who thought through their answers. I'm not suggesting you should try to determine if the person you are listening to is lying, but if the brain is fabricating what is true in any given moment to make sense of what is going on, then it serves you to listen beyond the person's words to discover the elements influencing his current interpretation of events. The results of Reinhard's research support the theory that judging inconsistencies, conflicting values, and justifications based on emotions are more accessible through intuitive processes than through the conscious mind.

To hear all the information you need for your Discomfort Zone conversation, you need to open yourself to receiving information with your entire nervous system. From your head, you can hear someone's faulty assumptions and beliefs. The processing of emotional reactions including fear, resistance, desires, and hopes happens in the entire nervous system, but primarily in the heart and gut. You "hear" different elements of a person's story from each of the processing centers:

+ Use your *head brain* to recognize the assumptions and beliefs that frame the person's story and to discern what is known from speculation to surface gaps in logic. You can also recognize rationalizations he uses to explain his decisions and actions to open the door to considering other viable options.

+ Use your *heart brain* to feel the energy found in yearning and passion, the sadness from loss, and the hesitation stemming from guilt. You can explore and acknowledge what you sense matters most and what feels wrong, off-center, or lost for him. You might also want to explore what is realistic versus idealistic about his desires, especially if he is beating himself up for not achieving something. Inquire about a commitment that seems to be lacking or a passion that has disappeared when you hear the words, "I should." If he feels overwhelmed, ask him to define his life's purpose or heart's desire instead of breaking down his tasks and priorities. Help him identify what his is worried about if he doesn't achieve his goals or dreams. Then discover what will happen when he does.

+ Use your *gut brain* to recognize what he has not been willing to call out that is keeping him from making a decision or moving forward. When his story keeps going in circles or he insists the change is too hard to make, explore what you feel he is protecting or clinging to and not wanting to let go of to move on. The loss he is afraid of facing could be anything— a friend, a job title, or his entire sense of self if he defines himself by his job or title. What will it take to let go and who will he be when he does? Ask him to explore what he will give up if he doesn't choose to act or think differently. Acknowledge the normality of his fears and confusion while challenging him to decide anyway, even if the decision is to wait instead of move.

Even if you are wrong about what you sense is blocking a person's movement or affecting his perception, you are helping him to think for himself at a deeper level. Share what you think you are sensing anyway. This will help him consider his own motivation more deeply. You need to share what you sense, explore what could be true, and challenge his resistance to create new frames and possibilities.

In order to listen at all three levels, you need to feel as if you are emotionally aligned from your head through your heart and down into the center of your body, your gut. Recall what you read in Chapter Two about being present mentally and emotionally to create your safety bubble. Practice your presencing routine.

Once you feel aligned and aware, you can use your breathing and feelings to open and listen from your three centers as you did in the previous exercise. The specific emotions to focus on are:

Head: curiosity

Heart: care or compassion

Gut: courage

When you consciously open all three of your processing centers with visualization and emotions, you are better able to sense what the person is not willing or unable to say. "I am not digesting this person" is the translation for a common Russian saying when one person doesn't understand the other. When you listen from all three processing centers, you are "fully digesting" the story beyond the words.

Partner Exercise in Three-Centered Listening

You will need to find someone to work with for this exercise. You will also need a timer you can easily start and stop so you don't have to worry about time while you are listening. Read the directions for each round to yourself before you start the timer and allow the other person talk.

If you can find a third person to work with you as a helper, have her read the directions for each round out loud to help you move your awareness into each part of your body. It is better to have the third person read the instructions so you as the listener can experience the shift instead of trying to read and feel at the same time. The three of you can then rotate after each cycle of three rounds, with each of you getting the chance to take on the role of the talker, the listener, and the helper/observer.

Throughout the exercise, the talker will be talking about one issue she is facing right now. It could be a new dilemma or a recurring source of frustration. The listener will be *sharing only one reflection and asking only one question* every two minutes based on what she hears when she listens primarily through a different part of her neural network. In fact, after the listener asks a question, the talker won't answer until the listener or helper resets the two-minute alarm for the next round. After you complete all three rounds, you can finish the conversation naturally.

Do not worry about whether you are doing the exercise correctly. It is more important that the person feels you are present and you care than how proficient your listening skills are. If you listen openly at these levels, you will get a good result. Do your best to fully engage in this exercise; whatever questions you ask are perfect for now.

Round 1 (Read first before listening)   The person will talk about her situation for two minutes. You will listen quietly from your head. Be curious. What do you want to know? What doesn't make sense? What pieces of the picture are missing? How does the person know if the reasons for her actions are sound? Listen for understanding and clarity. When the timer goes off after two minutes, you can make one reflective statement and ask one question. Do not say more than two sentences! Remember, your partner will not answer you until you are ready to start Round 2. Now set the alarm for two minutes and listen with curiosity from an open mind.

Round 2   Before your partner answers your Round 1 question, take a breath and clear your mind. Recall someone or something you deeply care about. See this person or thing you love. Take a deep breath in, smile, and say to yourself the word love, care, or gratitude. Feel your heart opening. Then when your partner speaks, silently listen for emotional cues. Is she excited? Resentful? Guilty? Worried? What does she want more than anything? What's getting in the way? Try to keep sensing from your heart without thinking. If you go back into your head, look at the person in front of you. Regard her as thou and feel compassion and care. Remember she is doing what she can to work through this issue. If you judge her, forgive yourself and reopen your heart to her words. When the timer goes off after two minutes, you can make one reflective statement and ask one question. Again, your partner will not answer until you are prepared to start Round 3. Now, reset your alarm for two minutes and listen from your open heart.

Round 3 Before your partner answers your Round 2 question, sit up straight and recall a time you felt gutsy and determined in spite of your fear. Recall how you felt as you took action or spoke your mind. As you inhale, say the word courage to yourself. Let the word settle into the core of your body just below your navel before you exhale. When you listen to your partner, receive the words, feelings, gestures, and pauses through your gut. What is she protecting? What is driving her choices? When the timer goes off after two minutes, make one reflective statement and ask one question. These statements may be more challenging than before. Be courageous. This time you can let your partner respond to your question after you ask it. Try to keep listening from your gut instead of returning to your head as you continue the conversation. Now, set your timer for two minutes and listen with strength from your gut.

Completion After you finish the conversation, take a few minutes to talk about the differences in your listening at each level and in the questions you asked. Ask your partner how she felt in each round to see if there were differences in the impact of your questions.

You might find you did well listening from two levels, but the third was not as accessible. Most of us are predominantly head thinkers. Yet listening from either the heart or gut might be easier for you than the other place. If you are a risk taker who moves quickly on instinct, you might find it easier to listen from your gut than your heart. Coming from your gut over your heart feels less vulnerable. Conversely, people who tend to be helpers listen more easily from their heart than their gut. The skill is to practice taking in impulses from the part of your body you're not used to so you can eventually balance your listening from all three centers.

Until your listening is open and balanced automatically, add a quick visualization to your presencing routine before you engage in a Discomfort Zone conversation. After you clear your mind and feel your body is relaxed, centered, and aligned with your intention for the conversation, close your eyes and visualize a bright golden ball in your brain. Say the word *curious* to yourself. Feel your mind open. Then smile, breathe into your chest, and watch the ball float down to your heart area. Say and feel the word *care* (or *love* if you dare) and feel your heart expanding. After a few relaxed breaths, inhale deeply into your abdomen as you watch the ball float down and stop just below your navel. Say and feel the word *courage*. Feel your gut open and ready to receive.

Open your eyes and look around the room keeping all three centers open. What details do you notice without thinking? What do you see and sense that you haven't noticed before? Are you able to go beyond seeing to observing as Sherlock Holmes suggested?

If the glowing orange ball doesn't work for you, then choose any visual that helps you shift your awareness from your head into your heart and gut. I worked with a sports psychologist who had his athletes visualize an elevator moving from the top of their heads down into their hearts and then gently stopping at a spot just below their navel. The elevator door opened at this spot but the cab was empty, waiting to receive. When the athletes returned to playing their sport, they attempted to keep their gut open and aware.

This practice will help you remove *I* from your conversation as you practiced in Chapter Two. We all have a tendency to slip into analysis and judgment. When you practice listening from your head, heart, and gut, you will be better at responding to what you are sensing instead of trying to lead the person toward your righteous conclusion.

To maximize your use of the Discomfort Zone, whenever the conversation feels uncomfortable for you, shift the balance to listening and speaking from your gut. You are less likely to censor your words from here. You will be better able to stay calm, silent, and determined when you listen and coach from your gut. In some martial arts, they call this your *point of strength*. With practice, you can learn to live from your point of strength as well.

Whenever a leader tells me that he couldn't get a conversation going, that the person he was speaking to was too resistant or unwilling to talk, I ask what was going on in his own head while trying to coerce the other person to speak. Generally, he will say he was stuck in his head brain, trying to figure out how to make the person more engaged in the conversation. People are much more willing to open up to you when they feel you are fully listening to them and responding from your heart and gut.

Remember, people are always telling you things they don't have words for in their tone, pauses, emotions, and omissions. When you listen to their stories through your heart and your gut, you can hear what they really want, need, or can't deal with. You're more likely to find the question that will break through the barrier protecting their reality. Excuses crumble. Blind spots come to light. Their awareness broadens. A new reality appears.

As I mentioned before, it can take time for a person to process the questions you ask. You may not get a breakthrough or "wow" moment in every conversation. The insight could come later or you may need a few conversations to build on smaller discoveries. I will share cases with you in the next two chapters in which the processing took different lengths of time.

How to Listen for What to Say

One final tip to remember: Sit up straight. Not only does hunching over and leaning toward someone crunch your gut, but there is evidence that people who are in a hunched posture for long periods are less assertive.Martin Bos and Amy Cuddy found that hunching over a smartphone screen or slouching over a laptop actually affects body chemistry and the willingness to be assertive.[8] They decided to do the research after they noticed how many people constrict their bodies over smartphones before attending meetings. Their research indicates a hunched-over posture could affect the courage available in subsequent conversations.

Check your posture as often as you can throughout the day. You will not only open your gut to receive more information, but you might be better at courageously challenging someone's thinking as well.

Feeling Stuck? Use Your Emotions to Move the Conversation Forward

Emotions are contagious. To create a safety bubble, you choose to be curious and caring as you hold the positive intention of helping the person see more broadly. From here, you might notice your emotions shift as you empathize with the person. You might share what you are feeling as part of the reflective process. Additionally, there are times when you may adjust your emotions to create either movement or closure in the conversation.

If the person keeps cycling back to the original story, you might breathe in a sense of calm resolve before you tell the person the pattern you are noticing in the conversation. Remind her of the desired outcome you agreed on (recall the DREAM model) and ask if she is willing to look at other ways of perceiving the situation so you can move into the reflection and exploration phases. If the person isn't happy about the awareness that has emerged, slip some hope into your words when you ask her to delineate the options she must choose from. If she realizes she must give up something to move forward, feel compassion as you allow her to grieve the loss or experience the regret. Then when she is willing to look at what comes next, feel your own courage as you encourage her to make a plan. The shift you make emotionally might be exactly what she needs to see through the darkness.

Humor can be used to lighten up the tone if you have established trust and you feel an appropriate opening. Shared laughter can relieve stress and boost self-confidence. Be judicious about how and when you use humor, however, so it is not seen as offensive or insensitive.

Humor tends to be spontaneous, so it is hard to teach when to use it. Usually, the person has had an epiphany and is ready to laugh at the old way she was interpreting a situation or sabotaging her own efforts. Or perhaps she just confessed to having a blind spot she should have seen a long time ago. Helping her laugh at herself can make the truth easier to admit. It is also possible you can demonstrate how laughing at yourself has helped you. When you sense she is ready to accept the truth but it feels a bit awkward, a brief funny example of your own *trip into the truth* can give her the nudge she needs. Remember to acknowledge her courage and insight before you wrap up the conversation.

Use your own emotions only when you feel a shift is needed to keep the conversation flowing. You don't want to interrupt when a person is processing a question you asked. Silence is more effective than trying to make someone feel better. Remember that silence isn't just shutting up. *Silence is holding a space of care and trust as a person's brain tries to make sense of what it is learning.*

Be sincere with any emotion you feel. You are not trying to manipulate the person to feel differently. You are shifting the conversation upward only when it is stuck or nearing the end.

Hopefully, the person will shift with you. Don't be discouraged if she doesn't. She may need you to quietly be with her where she is instead. Her sorrow, embarrassment, and frustration all indicate there is something important for her brain to consider.

The better you get at listening from your heart and gut as well as your head, the better you will know what the person needs from you emotionally as well as verbally. Trust the process. *And remember, the other person wants you to be present more than he or she needs you to be perfect.*

CHAPTER FOUR: Key Points to Remember

1. Sensing signals you receive from your heart and gut can be called *using your intuition*. This information is rapid, instinctual, and emotionally based. Reading these signals is crucial to successfully having a conversation in the Discomfort Zone.

2. You will pick up different cues when listening from your three processing centers: your head (reasoning/beliefs), your heart (values/desires), and your gut (protection/courageous impulses). When you listen from your head, heart, and gut, your reflections and questions are more spontaneous and profound.

3. To activate your three centers, you need to physically align your body. Ground yourself in the present moment and feel curious, compassionate, and courageous.

4. Try to keep your head, heart, and gut open and balanced while you listen. When you feel uncomfortable, however, speak and listen more deeply from your gut. When you feel impatient or begin to judge the person, focus on reopening your heart.

5. Use silence while a person's brain is hard at work trying to make sense of what has emerged. Use your emotions to uplift the tone of the interaction when it feels stuck or it is time for the person to make a commitment and end the conversation.

Chapter Five

New Perspective— Using Discomfort Zone Conversations to Break Through Barriers

"Nothing limits achievement like small thinking; nothing expands possibilities like unleashed imagination."

William Arthur Ward

In the winter of 2009, I attended the first European School of Management and Technology (ESMT) coaching colloquium in Berlin.[1] The theme of the colloquium was "Tricky Coaching: Difficult Cases in Leadership Coaching." In each case, the goals the client laid out at the start of the coaching engagement blurred over time. Resistance to change showed up in many ways. External circumstances had varying effects. There were numerous approaches the coach could have taken. There were no pat answers to any dilemma.

Each accepted case was sent to one or two other case authors to read and write an opinion on the coach's approach. When we came together in Berlin, we reviewed the cases and opinions, which inspired rich dialogue about the scenarios. Many of the cases have since been written into a wonderful book called *Tricky Coaching*.[2]

What turned out to be the most powerful part of the experience was the honest sharing among the participants as each confessed his or her own confusion, dissonance, and fears when faced with coaching dilemmas. Sharing cases provided potent learning. The colloquium gave us the opportunity to step back and consider difficult situations from numerous perspectives.

Therefore, I added cases to this book hoping you will not only reflect on them, but also discuss them with interested colleagues. The ability to examine cases while reflecting on your own past and present situations will help prepare you for dealing with the interpersonal subtleties you will encounter in the future. This book provides you with a framework and techniques for developing your skills, but because there is not one perfect path to follow to ensure success, these cases should help you think more broadly about your own conversations.

The following cases are from leaders who completed classes at the Healthcare Coaching Institute,[3] from public and corporate classes where I teach leadership skills, or from my individual work mentoring and coaching leaders to use the Discomfort Zone in their development conversations. The names, organizations, and industries have been changed to maintain confidentiality. In some cases, the characters and conversations were altered to ensure anonymity. The conversations were either taped or recalled soon after the session in an attempt to capture what occurred as much as possible. I chose situations that represent common situations leaders face. As they say in the movies, any resemblance to yourself or your clients in these cases is coincidental.

While reading the cases, notice what went well and consider what else could have worked if this were your scenario. What else might you say or ask that could lead to a different result? If you are one of a group of colleagues who meets to network and learn together, set up a time to examine and discuss the cases.

Map what transpired to the DREAM model. Listen to your heart and gut when discussing other possible approaches. Amazing wisdom emerges when studying the cases together. You will find more cases to review and comment on online at the website http://outsmartyourbrain.com/discomfort-zone-cases/

Diving into Resistance

The following three cases look at how the leaders initiating the conversations were able to break through well-established defense routines that were keeping the managers who reported to them or their colleagues from making changes or handling situations in the most productive way. The first case focuses on the manager's leadership style and what needs to expand to improve impact. The second case involves a top performer who was refusing to take responsibility for conflicts with her peers. In the third case, the person is having difficulties adapting to a new position.

The cases were chosen because they represent themes, patterns, challenges, and blind spots leaders typically need to address that could lead to breakthrough moments. Each case starts with some background information on the person being coached. Then after describing what happened that created a shift in thinking, each case ends with a few questions for you to reflect on to better apply the learning to your own situations.

Case 1 ■ I Get No Respect

Background

The senior manager, Martin, had been transferred to the region six months prior to the conversation. He had worked successfully as a manager in three other parts of the world and had worked for the company for fifteen years. In casual conversations, Martin was warm and amusing. When asked what type of leader he thought he was, he said he was definitely a people person and attributed much of his past success to his ability to connect with people.

The problem emerged not long after Martin arrived in his new position. Performance measures were mediocre in the region. People got their work done but not much more. He described the problem as cultural. The work ethic was low. Loyalty to the company was sparse. All the employees cared about was punching the clock and going for a beer before dinner.

Theme and Patterns

Confusing task management with leadership is common with even experienced, caring managers. Being *a people person* because you are approachable and an easy conversationalist is not enough to be effective as a leader. Sociable managers often assume their direct reports will come to them with problems and will be naturally motivated to give their best efforts because the manager created a pleasant work environment, attempted to know something about their employees' personal lives, and was patient when doling out goals and directions.

What's missing from this picture? Martin showed no curiosity about what his people need to feel inspired to give more time and energy to their work. Focusing only on finding ways to make it more enjoyable for people to work avoids the core of the problem—no one wants to work harder. You can't solve emotional and motivational issues by politely giving direction, bestowing praise, and knowing whose kids play soccer and whose play baseball. Nice managers can still entrench the lieutenant and his plebes mentality.

The pattern for this Discomfort Zone conversation between the manager and his leader starts with the manager either asking for support from his leader to exchange the old for new people or he tries to get the leader to agree that the problem is unsolvable because of cultural or situational factors. It is possible the manager hopes his leader will provide a magical solution that will resolve the problem, but usually the manager wants acknowledgment for doing everything right in a bad situation. This is the presenting situation whether the manager is a people person or an efficiency expert. The assumption is that the people are wrong and the manager, who has tried everything, is right. If there is a solution, though the manager doubts one exists, it is external to the manager. If only the people worked harder and cared more, everything would be okay.

Challenge for the Leader Holding the Conversation

The desired outcome is always owned by the person in front of you, not by anyone else. The stated request was to find ways to motivate unmotivated employees. Yet the cynicism in the manager's voice reflects surety that the situation is cultural and unchangeable with the current work team. Regardless of whether this is true or not, the leader needs to listen for the block to success as the manager tells the story. The focus of the conversation should not be on the manager's employees; it should be on the manager's blind spots. Therefore the reflection and exploration would focus on what the manager is doing, who he thinks he is in the situation in terms of his role, and what he might be doing to actually intensify, not alleviate, the resistance the workers are demonstrating. Otherwise, no solution will produce significant and long-lasting results.

Always allow the person to vent at the beginning of the conversation to help create the connection and safety bubble. Even if you have seen this problem a hundred times before, you need to acknowledge the disappointment and anger your manager feels. The truth about what is creating the difficulty will surface inside the complaints. Often a good dose of reflection—allowing the manager to hear his own words—will shine a light on what is wrong with his approach. Then you can address the conflict in how his current approach contradicts how he wants to be seen by his direct reports.

In this situation, as the manager described the work habits of his people, his disdain grew. The angrier he got, the more he revealed his pattern for constantly giving directions and explanations about how work should get done, which also implied that many of his conversations with his reports were focused on what people were doing wrong. He wasn't the light-hearted, praise-giving person he described himself to be.

When you sense anger and frustration, listen with your heart. When explaining the situation, the manager expressed both disappointment and frustration because his direct reports didn't appreciate what he thought he was doing for them. In turn, the hearts of his employees were hardened from neglect. The questions that emerge from listening with your heart could provide the key to what the manager needs to shift the situation.

Breakthrough Moment

It would be easy to fall into the trap of telling Martin how to change his behavior to get different results. This approach will likely solidify his cynicism even though he is asking for suggestions. He could find fault with the suggestions or say he has tried them already, giving him even more validation that he has tried everything short of changing people and assignments.

Neurologist, psychiatrist, and Holocaust survivor Viktor Frankl said, "When we are no longer able to change a situation, we are challenged to change ourselves." In this case, the leader holding the conversation was a woman who managed Martin from another country. She headed up a large division of the organization spanning many countries. Because Martin was new to his position, he had only a few meetings with her prior to this conversation.

The breakthrough moment came in the conversation when, after listening to the story, the leader asked Martin with heart-felt sincerity, "You say you are a people person. Would your current direct reports describe you that way?"

The question clearly surprised Martin. He blindly stared as his brain searched for an answer. After a long pause, he said, "I would like them to, but I'm not sure what they think of me the way things have been going."

The leader then reflected, "You've taken steps to show you care. But you are in the dark knowing what makes them care."

"True."

"If you want your organization to change, what are you willing to change about yourself?"

"I don't know."

"That's a great place to start, not knowing what to do. How can you find out?"

Martin gave the pat answer, "I guess I can ask them." The leader didn't leave the conversation there, however. She explored what asking his reports would look like, covering both individual and team meetings.

Then the conversation shifted to motivation. The leader said, "I know you work hard. You're a self-starter. You don't need much to feel motivated. When you think about the leaders you have had in the past, what did they do to inspire you? Has anyone done something that made you feel good about who you are, not just the work you do?"

Martin related moments in which his own leaders challenged him to take on new tasks and roles, which helped him to feel like a significant player on a team that had a clear and important purpose. They also ensured he had the resources to succeed in his own way.

As a result, Martin realized that being a people person wasn't enough to be a good leader. He committed to meeting with each of his team members to talk about the significance of their work, what they felt was their purpose, and what they hoped for in their careers whatever that might be. He also clarified the new perspective, attitude, and mindset he would use while having these conversations.

Reflection Questions

Look at what worked in the conversation. What emotions, unspoken needs, and blind spots did the leader pick up? In your point of view, what did the leader miss? What other reflection and questions would you use? Do you think this is a good example or did you find the solution too simple? If so, how do you see this scenario playing out if you were the leader? Consider these questions on your own or find someone to discuss them with. In addition, when a person you work with is stuck blaming others for a problem, consider these questions:

1. What need is not getting met? What is he angry about, frustrated with, or hurt by in the situation? How do the circumstances threaten his self-concept?

2. How might his self-concept be in conflict with how others see him? Does he act differently when stressed or confused than what he claims would be ideal behavior? Who does he become when he isn't well received?

3. What does he need to let go of in order to move on? Do you think the person knows what he needs to do but is resisting, or is this truly a blind spot beyond his awareness? Explore both possibilities.

Remember not to try to replicate this conversation. Even if you use similar questions, the timing for asking questions is critical. The questions you ask must be in response to what is said, using the words of the person telling the story.

Case 2 ■ No One Cares Like I Do

Background

Reva wanted a promotion. Her work produced stellar results. She had moved to a different country and had mastered the language, the culture, and the increased responsibilities. Her leader couldn't argue that she had excellent work skills, but said he couldn't promote her until she improved her relationships with her peers. Her colleagues frequently complained to him about her condescending tone and unrequested advice. Her manager had also witnessed the way she corrected and admonished her peers openly in meetings.

The situation is similar to the first case in that Reva feels she is spending too much time getting others to work harder and better. In this case, the people with the low work values and ethics are her peers instead of subordinates.

Her manager asked me to coach her, but instead I offered to coach him on how to have a Discomfort Zone conversation with Reva. The conversation described in the Breakthrough Moment section is based on what he, as the leader, wrote up for me after he spoke with her and got her permission to share the case. From the changes in Reva's subsequent behavior, I believe the case was accurately reported.

Theme and Patterns

Most high achievers and young leaders tend to manage up and down but not sideways, even though they need the respect and support of their peers to succeed.[4] They neglect these relationships either for lack of time or because they feel the need to compete with and outshine their peers. Neglect due to time constraints is often an oversight that can be fixed with deliberate action. Tempering a sense of competition or superiority is more difficult to address.

High achievers often grow up being praised for being the smartest kids in the classroom. This recognition might be wonderful for their self-esteem, but it doesn't teach collaboration. Visibly ranking children can embed a sense of competition such that the top children feel the need to continue outdoing their peers to hold the position of preeminence. It also doesn't teach kids to have empathy for those who aren't the smartest in the room. When the children grow up, they often demonstrate an attitude at work that reflects, "If you can't do what I do then you will always produce inadequate results."[5] Couple this with the contradiction that the high achiever might not want anyone to perform better at her level, she is then constantly burdened with proving her greatness at the expense of teamwork. To change, the high achiever needs to see that supporting instead of quarreling with one's teammates will help her achieve her long-term goals and, possibly, the results will be more purposeful and satisfying.

The pattern for this Discomfort Zone conversation starts with the person either resisting the need to change because her work yields the best results and everyone else's performance is substandard, or she claims she can't change who she intrinsically is or she would be acting inauthentically. As in Case 1, the blame is on everyone else. If only other people worked harder and cared more, everything would be okay. In this situation, the person also believes the leader should be tougher on her peers instead of expecting her to give in and play nicely.

Challenge for the Leader Holding the Conversation
For a change to be genuine and lasting, the person needs to want to improve because it is the right thing to do, not because there

will be a reward. Often, the person believes that if he or she will be more tolerant of others, there will be a reward for good behavior. He will get a better performance review. She will earn a promotion. There must, however, be a corresponding change in work values and attitude, not just actions. Solutions focused only on using different interpersonal skills will not ensure a long-term change.

To change the person's mind, the conversation needs to focus on personal identity and purpose. An expansion of these frameworks will cause a more significant and long-lasting shift in behavior. When you as a leader can assist someone to explore who she could be as a human and a leader in various communities instead of who she is as an achiever who excels, there is a chance she will expand her sense of self in relationships. When you can guide her to declare a purpose that is bigger than her own achievements, there is a chance she will broaden her view of the world and the people she works with.

Challenge the person to improve the present situation so she doesn't re-create the problem elsewhere. It will be easy for the high achiever to blame the problem on the current team. If you hear this when she talks—that she believes she would thrive in a different culture or with a team of A-players somewhere else—call it out. Whether or not this is true, if there is a desire to be a leader, this is the perfect challenge to resolve. If she runs from it, the problem will continue to haunt her relationships. If instead she triumphs in her current situations, she will change her sense of self and behaviors forever. She will know what it feels like to be a leader who helps others instead of just being an achiever who excels.

Speak from your gut to match her intensity. High achievers tend to be passionate people who are both bold and determined. Their spirit is exemplary. To break through their barriers, you need to be strong with your feedback, questions, and requests. You also need to be clear and to the point to earn their respect early on. Heart-felt appeals about the right thing to do or how much you care about their stress levels will get an "I know, I know" response and not much more. When in a Discomfort Zone conversation, you are the person's thinking partner; be as direct and bold as she is to unlock her brain.

Breakthrough Moment

During the Discomfort Zone conversation with her leader, the two words that triggered Reva were *power* and *mission* as they related to her desire to be a leader. Her manager started the conversation declaring the intention of wanting to help her reach her goal of earning a promotion. He trusted her in every way except for one— her ability to influence and inspire her peers. He didn't state this gap as a need for her to get along with or even tolerate her peers. He said that one of the measurements of leadership in the company was the ability to align with and inspire others at all levels of the organization. He needed to see evidence that she was up for this challenge.

He then shifted the conversation to explore her sense of identity at work by asking her what she felt her purpose was now and how it might shift if she were given the promotion. The force of her words was strong. Her passion for excellence resonated from her gut.

The moment of truth came when her leader said, "You are a strong, smart woman. Your focus on excellence is admirable. I believe you could have a lot of power. But how you show your desire to have others work harder and more efficiently feels more like force than power. What would it take for your peers to admire you, so they see you as a powerful leader who stands up for them instead of just a strong woman?"

She said, "I always thought power . . ." She paused, inhaled deeply, and let out her breath before she replied, "I need to stop fighting."

"Maybe help them win their battles instead of causing the battle yourself?"

"Yes, I see. Okay, I could find out what they think is causing them problems and help them solve them so they don't see me as competition."

"So you will tell them what to do. You will fix their problems."

"No, no. That hasn't worked. If I have a good idea, I need to create a vision they can see and want. A little salesmanship could help."

Her boss asked, "Would you like to restate your purpose and mission?"

She agreed and stated that she truly wanted for her peers to see her as a leader. She didn't want to give up striving for excellent results, but she felt if she could inspire everyone to work together as a team, she would deserve the honor of being their leader.

Her boss didn't accept her solution as final. He asked, "Why should I believe in you?"

"What do you mean?"

"You haven't wanted to do this before. Why now?"

"I want to be seen as a leader."

"Yes, but will you feel like a leader if you do this?"

"I feel a little like I'm giving in to them."

"Are you?"

"Yes and no, but I don't know what I will feel until I try. I'm sure if things start to change, I'll believe it more. You know, believe it when you see it. Can we revisit the situation once I give it a good try?"

"How long is a good try?"

"A few months, I think."

"We have a meeting on the books every month as I do with the entire team. But if it gets discouraging, you'll let me know right away, okay?

"Okay, but I want to set up meetings with each of my peers to see what they are working on and how I can help. They might not trust me."

They talked about what it would take for Reva to gain the trust of her peers during team meetings and through informal one-on-one *get to know you* conversations over lunch. Her leader closed out the conversation by affirming his belief in her and offering his support however she needed it.

In a subsequent conversation, Reva told her boss she realized if she were truly committed to improving the bottom line, she needed to focus on relationships as well as results. She agreed to ask her peers for their feedback as well as ideas, including their evaluation of her leadership. This would definitely take courage. She also said she was working hard to manage her emotions and reactions in her meetings, asking herself, "What would a leader do?" when she questioned her colleague's contributions. Her boss told me he felt more comfortable recommending her for a promotion when the opportunity arose.

Reflection Questions

Again, look at what worked in the conversation. What emotions, unspoken needs, and blind spots did the leader pick up? In your point of view, what did the leader miss? What other reflection and questions would you use? Do you think this is a good Discomfort Zone example or did you find the solution too simple? If so, what would you do differently?

In addition, if you are working with someone who is struggling with relationships because he or she judges others too harshly, consider these concepts as you listen:

1. What values are framing the person's self-concept? How do her work values define who she thinks she is and what she believes is her mission at work? How does

her mission make other people feel? Is it oppressive or inspiring? Does her mission match her work description or her aspirations?

2. How does she define *power*? When considering her relationships with her own managers, what use of power does she most appreciate? Does she believe the use of power can be inspiring instead of domineering? What feels uncomfortable to her about using power this way?

3. In order to let go of being the Superstar or Hero, what must she give up? What title could she give herself instead that would help her feel good about letting go of a part of her identity that has defined her for years?

Remember to give the person space to feel uncomfortable with new ways of being with others. It's likely she will feel awkward in her first attempts to change her behavior. She will need your support to maintain her commitment through times of stress and doubt.

Case 3 ■ Been There, Loved That, Now What?

Background

This case is about the reality of making a major professional transition. Although the case identifies a specific situation, the themes, patterns, and breakthrough moment could be the same for anyone who is moving on from a significant role in his or her life whether by personal choice or forced by the organization, family, or health issues.

John worked for a large corporation that had a tradition of rotating technical specialists into key decision-making positions for a set period of time. Some of the specialists could opt to be developed for higher leadership positions. Yet even these positions had *term limits* so the person holding a position was moved to

New Perspective

another position every four years, if not earlier. John had taken on a number of leadership responsibilities before he was tapped to lead an entire division. He held the position for twelve years, three times longer than others holding his or similar positions. The exception had been made as the division faced two back-to-back recessions and a number of large change initiatives. John successfully led his organization through these storms.

When the time finally came for John to move on, he and the employees of his division reluctantly accepted the decision for him to step down. John opted for his next position to be within the Leadership Development team, where he would mentor and coach others as they moved into leadership positions. This was the likely transition because more than a decade had passed since John worked as a specialist. Plus, he had accumulated a wealth of wisdom and perspective to share with younger leaders.

John came to the conversation with the goal of improving his listening and coaching skills. He knew coaching would be critical to help young leaders think for themselves. Also, when they faced a crisis, he would not be there to tell them what to do.

However, John felt that not only did he struggle asking questions, he didn't seem to listen very long before he came up with a brilliant solution. He just couldn't break his habit of immediately formulating and giving someone an answer, but he wanted to change.

Theme and Patterns

Mythologist Joseph Campbell said, "We must let go of the life we have planned, so as to accept the one that is waiting for us." An intentional transformation—one you direct instead of feeling forced to make—requires that you clearly see what you must release. From this vantage point, it is easier to step into the next phase even if you still need to grieve for what you are letting go.

One of my former clients was trying to shift to teaching after being a paramedic. She had developed rheumatoid arthritis and could no longer perform out in the field. The overarching question became, "How do you create a life that feels fulfilling after one that felt amazing?"

The shift is particularly difficult when the person was in the spotlight and now has the role of helping others to be in the spotlight. The values must shift from *I do great work (for my organization, my team, my family, my community, or all humanity)* to *they do great work*. Leaders will witness the attachment to *I* at many levels in the people they work with, whether someone is moving into their first leadership position after being a superstar performer or a leader needs to step back toward the end of a brilliant career. A transition could take place at any time for family or health reasons as well.

Typically, successful senior leaders are independent and decisive people who get things done, especially in fast-paced, chaotic organizations. So it can be unnerving to step into being supportive, patient, and committed to helping others make decisions on their own. They know they miss things by not listening fully. They know they are not serving the young, smart leaders by trying only to instruct them. Yet without having a strong emotional reason to change their style, they rarely succeed in fully making the transition.

The pattern for the Discomfort Zone conversation starts with the person either beating himself up for not being perfect in his new role or already identifying the solution to the problem— he knows what to do but just needs to be more disciplined. In this case, John blames himself for what he considers a personal failure. However, blaming himself for his mistakes and taking full responsibility for making the career transition are two different things. John needs to recognize the strength of the

New Perspective

attachment he still has to the way it used to be and who he once was. Then he needs to see this attachment as a detriment if he is to fully accept the new role he is in.

Challenge for the Leader Holding the Conversation

Don't get sucked into a problem-solving conversation. It's likely the smart person in front of you knows what needs to be done but is not yet willing to temper his ego to change his behavior. He may still long for his old position and the glory he received. He will tell you why it's so hard to change. He will tell you how badly he feels about not being able to do what he knows he is supposed to do. He will ask, sometimes beg, for your suggestions. It will be easy for you to slide into a comfortable conversation looking at skill-building techniques, the value of changing, and the consequences for not succeeding. He will agree. He might even come up with a brilliant idea that will help him in the future and thank you profusely.

Don't buy it.

He must let go of being the *one who knows* or the *one who saves the day.*

Therefore, before moving forward to finding solutions, let the person express what it was like to be in his previous position. Let him bask in his memories. Get him to tell you how important he was and what wonderful outcomes he achieved. Then he may see why it is so hard to let go.

If the new who is not as powerful as the old who, the shift might not take place. Once he reveals his glorious past, you can look to see if there is anything as important or wonderful for him going forward. How will he continue to feel as relevant as before? If he can't imagine a future that feels powerfully significant, he may not be able to make the transition.

Do not dismiss the possibility that the other person might be better off re-creating his old position somewhere else if he is not ready to move on. Doing something he is supposed to do without passion could be a lose-lose scenario. Yes, he probably needs to give the new position a fighting chance before he decides to look elsewhere. He should not decide he is failing because he isn't perfect. If, however, he can't find fulfillment as he becomes proficient in the new role, the loss of confidence and self-worth might be overwhelming.

If he is adamant about making the shift, he will need to accept the past as over before he can move on to his next phase in life.

Accepting the past is over is an emotional process. Regardless of how good it is to devote more time to developing others, to family, or even to one's own health, saying good-bye to a fulfilling past is sad work. The moment a person recognizes what he has lost will be painful. He might need to take a break from the conversation to think. Honestly, he needs to grieve. If you are listening from your heart and gut, you will know when it is time to back off. Acknowledge his discovery as a powerful revelation. Ask how you can best support him. If he wants to take time to think, set a time to meet again.

Be firm and compassionate when helping people see they are holding on to mere memories. Although this conversation might become a familiar pattern for you if your job is to develop leaders or oversee organizational changes, the conversation will be different with each person you face. The dance to protect the ego will differ each time. You won't be able to ask the same questions every time to get the results you want. Stay present so you can stay anchored in the process. Frame your reflections and questions with the words they use and the emotions they express. Otherwise, you will have logic-based conversations that do not reveal the core of the problem.

Stay steady with your inquiry. The ego-protecting barrier will be strong. You need to break through it to help the person move on.

New Perspective

Breakthrough Moment

During the conversation, John quickly realized his desired outcome of the conversation had nothing to do with skill improvement. He knew what skills he needed to develop, he knew the benefits if he performed the skills well, and he knew he could enjoy his new role. When he got impatient and didn't listen, he beat himself up for failing, which didn't feel good. With the facts on the table, John recognized it was time to identify what had been stopping him from moving forward.

John described his current technique by saying, "I really have to be intentional when I am coaching. I have to tell myself, 'Question, question. Ask two in a row. Ask three in a row before you give your opinion about what you think.' It's hard work."

The leader replied, "It sounds like you are biding your time before you can do what you really want to do—give your opinion."

"I want to get better at this."

"I know you think that. It doesn't feel to me that you really believe it."

"Of course I believe it or I wouldn't try."

"John, I know you believe that there is a right way to be successful in the role you are in now. I feel there is something else at play here than just whether you can ask a few more questions before you respond. Giving your opinion still feels like the priority, that you are asking questions just to get to that moment."

"Okay, so I'm not doing it right. What am I missing?"

"What is really making this so hard for you?"

"I have opinions. My opinions kick in a little early. That's part of it. When people start talking about what is bothering them, I know I've been there and want to give them an answer rather than probing why it is important to them. It's hard to turn that off. I suppose once you are in a senior leadership position and then move on, it's just hard. And for me, I'm still in the same organization, which is rare."

"How do people there see you now?"

After a long pause, John started speaking quickly. "To be honest, I enjoyed my job very much. When we moved into a growth period, it was fun. I knew the day would come that it would end, but I wasn't ready. Anyway, the organization moves people around for good reason."

"So how are you important now?"

John averted his gaze, and then looked up and around as if searching for the answer. Then he looked down and quietly said, "I'm still playing the role. They are letting me do it. Theoretically, I should be able to turn that off. But then, I don't know."

"Would you like to talk about what's possible in your new role?"

"I guess I am in a transition in life I don't quite understand. I know there are good things happening with my family, with the leadership development, and all that I can give back. But I miss some of the old stuff."

"Have you made any significant transitions before?"

John talked about the difficult transition he had to make from being a technical expert to becoming a leader. In the middle of his story, he said, "You know, I have to write this down. That was really powerful."

The leader gave John a moment to make his note before saying, "From my point of view, you are continuing to do phenomenal work. And your willingness to be vulnerable and learn will help all the leaders you touch. What a powerful role you now have."

"I'm beginning to see that."

"But can you trust it? You aren't just applying skills. You are changing who you think you are. You have been pulled out of one frying pan and slapped into another. You are still making a difference, which you said is most important. When you let go of who you once were, you might be able to fully breathe in how amazing the next phase of your career truly is. What else can I do to support you?"

John said he needed time to reflect on the conversation. The next time the two met, they discussed the slow but consistent letting go process. They also discussed the greater ease John was feeling around helping others think through their dilemmas instead of feeling the need to jump in with his opinions. He admitted that he wasn't perfect, but he wasn't beating himself up so much for his mistakes. He was finally looking forward to his future.

Reflection Questions

Do you think this is a good example of helping a person make a career transition or did you find the solution too simple? If so, how do you see this scenario playing out? What would you have done differently? Consider these questions on your own or find someone to discuss them with you:

1. In any forced transition, what is the motivation to change? What is the motivation not to change? What would the person have to acknowledge or release in order to find fulfillment with a new sense of self?

2. Is it possible that the person believes his current way of doing things is the best way even if he were told he had to change? If so, will he be able to make the change or will he sabotage his own efforts if he doesn't fully commit to making the transition? You have to get to the bottom of what he truly believes before you can look at what else is possible.

3. Does the person really want the position he has moved into? He may not be able to answer this until he fully lets go of who he was in the past. If, however, he no longer talks about going back to something, you might be able to focus the conversation on what is working now, what is not working, and what he can envision for his future.

Remember—*all career and life transitions are gradual processes, not instantaneous events.*[6] Where is the person on the continuum between letting go of the past and stepping into the unknown future? Courage is needed throughout the process. This is primarily a gut-based conversation for both of you. You can engage a person's heart to dream once he or she is courageous enough to let go of the past.

Chapter Six

Transformation— Using Discomfort Zone Conversations to Embrace What's Next

"If you do not change direction, you may end up where you are heading."
Lao Tzu

When I announced to my friends I wanted to be a public speaker, one woman suggested I take improvisational acting classes to improve my spontaneity and presence on the stage. I attended a workshop. Although my "I'm no actor" brain hated many of the exercises, the moments I felt free to talk and behave without care were exhilarating.

For the following two years, I flew to Los Angeles for a weekend workshop every three months. We were rarely instructed to be funny when given scenarios to play out, but many of my classmates were delightfully hilarious. I preferred to be dramatic.

One weekend, the instructor pulled me aside and requested I lighten up for the day. When I asked for clarification, she suggested I refrain from saying anything intelligent or profound. I should just be ordinary, even boring.

"Boring?" I asked. "I work so hard at being interesting and motivational."

"That's the problem," she replied, "People think you say smart things. They are impressed, but you don't change their lives. They don't see you or feel you. And they have no sense they are like you at all. Let them in by just being you. I've seen you talking with people in the hallway. You're pretty funny and accessible when you aren't being so smart."

I felt hurt, but even more, I was angry. Funny? I wasn't a comedian. I didn't see myself as an entertainer. How could I be something I wasn't? I started planning my escape out the side door.

Before I could wriggle away from her, she took me by the arm and walked me up on stage. She told the class I was the first performer in the next exercise. Then she gave us a series of unfinished statements we had to complete as honestly as we could as we took turns on stage. The statements were to tell people where we were born and why, where we grew up and why, where we live now and why, and where we would probably die and why. I shared my locations and rationale in a monotone with no color or cleverness.

For some reason, the laughs grew with every statement I made. When I got to the part of where I thought I would be laid to rest, the class was roaring before I could finish. I stared, not knowing what to say. My incredulous look seemed to top off my performance. The applause was so astounding I finally smiled.

The teacher, who had been standing near me the entire time, took my hand and said in my ear, "You can never tell yourself that lie again."

Whether she signaled for the class to laugh at me or not, my sense of *who I am* and *what I do* changed forever. The person I thought I should be disappeared. The work I thought I should be doing took on a new form. Not only was I free to be funny—to bring humor to daily dilemmas and gracefully lighten up serious situations—I was able to connect with people more readily. My teacher broke through my all-knowing veneer. I was able to establish trust and intimacy in my coaching and from the stage.

As a leader, you will encounter many people who need to be set free. They are prisoners of a sense of self that is confining, of work that is not enjoyable, and possibly of a life they did not consciously choose. If part of your job is to help these people succeed, then exploring what success means to them personally is vital. You must ask yourself if is it your responsibility to help people succeed where they are today or to help them discover where they can best succeed even if it means making changes you didn't expect. When you see someone struggling with making an important decision that will impact his or her future, do you know how to keep your own perspective, opinions, and desires for that person out of the way so you can help her discover what she truly wants for herself?

If you are willing to hold conversations with people about *who* they are in their work, what is stopping them from reaching their highest potential, and what they need to feel fulfilled in their lives, you are doing your best service as a leader. This puts you in the category of *transformational* instead of *transactional* leader.[1] Being a *transformational* leader increases productivity and bottom line results whether people decide to stay or go because the motivation to succeed is internally based on individual growth not externally based on organizational goals.

Expanding *Who I Am*

Whereas the previous chapter focused on breaking through the walls of resistance to recognize performance-detracting blind spots, this chapter explores ways of helping people break down how they currently frame *who they are* at work so they can create a new sense of self going forward.

Whether a person is successful or not in the present moment, clinging to a role, lifestyle, and identity is confining. The challenge is to establish enough safety in the conversation so the person feels she can explore her frustrations, her fears, and what she honestly wants from life.

There will be discomfort in these conversations, for both of you. In the process, you might break through your own boundaries of who you think you are as a leader. The moment you witness someone realizing she is free to choose what is right for herself, especially when she had no idea what options existed before the conversation began, could transform your own meaning of *leadership* forever.

The first case looks at a woman who can't seem to get anyone at work to implement her marketing strategy. The second case involves a man who is positioning himself for a promotion but can't earn favor from his manager. This case will include a contrasting situation with a woman who has been offered a dream job she is afraid of taking. In the third case, the person took a leap of faith that now feels like a failing endeavor.

Remember to notice what went well in the conversations and consider what else could have worked if this were your scenario. What else might you say or ask that could lead to a different result? Consider how your own situations—past, present, and future—might relate to these scenarios. If you have the opportunity to discuss the cases with your colleagues, explore how to use the insights that emerge to guide your next Discomfort Zone conversations.

Case 1 ▪ Square Peg in a Round Hole

Background

Dawn oversees business processes in a forty-employee retail business owned by her and her husband. She laid out a plan for a new customer service strategy that required buy-in by the four managers in the company. Everyone has excuses for not doing what she asked. She is frustrated.

Dawn joined her husband in the business a few years ago after being laid off from a large scientific research company going through economic difficulties. She had held leadership positions for fifteen years prior to this transition. She loved her work and felt she could bring a wealth of experience with her to help her husband grow the company.

Now three years into the job, she feels her husband never fully backs her ideas. He said he liked her current plan but won't address the resistance the managers show to executing it. This is not the first time she has experienced this situation. She has struggled to implement anything substantial. Her frustration is beginning to affect her relationship with her husband outside of work as well as during their daily workplace squabbles.

The culture of the company is very much like a family. Many of the employees have been with the business since they graduated from high school. The business has a good reputation for quality in the community. Her husband has made very few changes in business processes over the years. The business has experienced stability through all the economic highs and lows but little growth. Dawn thought she and her husband had agreed that the time was right to grow the business. That is her mission.

Dawn came to the conversation looking for advice on how to hold people accountable to execute her strategy. The four managers in the company had not been arguing with her about the legitimacy of her ideas but never get around to implementing them. She didn't know if the problem is their resistance to change or her lack of authority.

Theme and Patterns

It is very common for leaders and superstars in one situation to want to transfer their successful ways to new jobs. In fact, the new division or company is fertile ground to build on what has worked well for a person before. Never mind the person has landed in a culture that is different, the problems aren't the same, and people aren't ready to follow someone new to their tribe.

It is possible the Discomfort Zone conversation could focus on what the person thinks the new role is compared to what everyone else thinks. There could be a breakthrough when the person realizes the real reason no one is doing *the right things* has to do with his or her own ability to influence based on both a lack of authority and a lack of belonging. Then the person might be open to determining how to become one of the tribe instead of being an arrogant alien. From that position, he or she might eventually earn the respect needed for authentic followership.

Also, as in Dawn's situation, people often take on roles that *seem to be* a natural progression when the roles don't turn out to feel natural or fulfilling at all. Then they bang their heads against the wall trying to succeed instead of looking for a better fit elsewhere. Dawn loved working in a corporation where she ran a big team. She loved working in the sciences. She loved having budgets to try out new things. She is no longer there.

Dawn initially wanted her leadership coach to help her discover a new way to deal with the resistant managers. With reflection, exploration, and acknowledgment, that goal evolved into identifying how she could best contribute to any company and to herself. Dawn then made a commitment to begin her search for a new, more fulfilling job.

Challenges for the Leader Holding the Conversation

Persistence is not always a virtue. Persistence is needed for mastery; it is not always needed when making life decisions. People will come to you for help with their problems. Remember to look for all the blocks and reasons they give for not moving forward before you assume they just need a new skill or a strategy to resolve their issues.

The question here is more about what Dawn truly wants from her work. What circumstances contribute to her sense of significance? When is work most meaningful and fulfilling for her? When you help a person define what she needs to thrive, you are better able to help the person assess if the position she is in is a good fit or not.

People often climb a corporate ladder because it is the next rung to step on, not because it fulfills their needs. Or they take on a new challenge without assessing if the situation is amenable to their style and ideas. They might even choose a job or career path because other people tell them it's a good idea. These well-meaning people can be parents, bosses, teachers, colleagues, or spouses who want them to be happy. People even heed advice from strangers before they trust what their hearts are crying for them to do.

Be careful not to jump to finding solutions too quickly. When someone asks for help, it is easy to move into discussing action alternatives, which could lead to settling on a temporary fix. Then you miss the key information that identifies the real block to moving forward. Remember to look at the assumptions a person may be making about the situation, expectations that are creating disappointment and frustration, and fears and worries about the future. Go below the surface to get a clearer view of what the person wants and needs. With your reflections and exploring questions, the person can then determine what is best for her in the future and what is achievable now.

When you become bored or frustrated with a person's stories, take this as an indication she needs a push. Circular stories and excuses are signs she isn't taking personal responsibility for the untenable situation or she is avoiding an action that requires courage. Break the cycle by sharing what you are experiencing and ask her to name an action she would be willing to take no matter who is at fault. You might have her review a number of possible choices but make sure she commits to taking one.

Breakthrough Moment

A personal breakthrough came when Dawn realized what she wanted was not possible in the position she held. For many reasons, she thought working with her husband was a good choice. Three years later she has no real authority in the company, and the only recognized leader (her husband) doesn't want to change. An even greater realization came when Dawn finally felt free enough to talk about what she didn't like about the business. This led her to recognizing where she really wanted to be when she dressed and drove to the place she called work.

Dawn loved creating strategic plans with a team that would impact many people. She loved designing and implementing procedures that would increase efficiency as well as results. She felt her work was significant when the company provided a product that helped save lives. She was deluding herself to think she could apply even a fraction of what she loved about her expertise to a small, conventional company that offered a useful but not lifesaving service.

The breakthrough moment came when the leadership coach shifted the conversation from the implementation problem to focusing on what Dawn was really angry about.

"Dawn, do you think no one wants to implement your ideas because they don't like them or because your husband won't support your authority to implement them?"

"Probably both, but if he supported me it would be easier to hold people accountable."

"Is that what you are most upset about, that your husband didn't live up to your expectations?"

"Maybe. Huh. He is who he is."

"Then who is disappointing you?"

She contemplated the question for a moment before she shrugged her shoulders.

"Step back for a moment. If the company were a board game, where are you in relationship to everyone else?"

She paused as she formulated the picture in her mind. "I'm not even on the board. I'm out of the game."

"It doesn't mean that your intention and strategies aren't good."

"I know, but I'm beating a dead horse here."

"So what about that makes you angry?"

"I'm in my fifties and I don't enjoy getting out of bed every day."

The conversation shifted to Dawn sharing what she had hoped she could do for the business based on what she loved to do in the past. That didn't happen, leaving her to feel trapped in a job that had little substance for her other than helping to support her household. She was still angry with her former company for laying her off, angry she had settled for a less than fulfilling job, and angry no one appreciated what she could do.

"So Dawn, who is trapping you?"

This was the real breakthrough moment. After a long silence, Dawn quietly explained she was holding on to a belief that her illustrious career was over and her job was to help herself and her husband move toward retirement. Once she spoke this truth, she could see how unhappy she was playing out this story.

With this revelation, Dawn's mind opened and she could see other possibilities for herself. She designed clear actions to systematically free herself from her job while not impacting the business operations. The first step was to work with her husband to hire a general manager to offload some of her responsibilities.

With more free time, Dawn is pursuing learning opportunities and volunteer work while she considers possible jobs in larger corporations that would welcome her years of experience and passion for excellence. The burden has been lifted. She is free to find her way.

Reflection Questions

Do you think the conversation took the right path or would you have dug deeper to find ways Dawn could have made her current situation work better? What would you have done differently? Consider these questions on your own or work through them with a colleague or group:

1. When someone is complaining, what could be causing the person to feel angry, hurt or betrayed? What expectations did he or she have that were not met? Once a person begins to identify her emotions, she might unearth the real reasons she is upset.

2. If there were a magical fix for everything she is complaining about, what could it achieve? Are there other ways to achieve these results or is it time to recalibrate and move on? Maybe she needs to know it's okay to admit she made a wrong decision. Persistence can blind people to the need to do something else.

3. Does the person need to be given permission to dream? Dreams die out when hope is lost. When you encourage someone to envision a new future, you spark the

excitement of possibility. This spark is life force. What questions can you ask that might fuel the force of the life for someone whose light has dimmed?

Case 2 ▪ What Is at Stake Here, Really?

Background

Eric saw himself as the rising star of his organization, but he was recently turned down for a promotion he thought should have been his. He is great at resolving customer issues, establishing good relationships with the stakeholders important to his entire team, and creating brilliant sales presentations.

He thinks his boss sabotaged his chances. On Eric's last performance review, his boss rated him as *exceeding expectations* on all of his objectives except one—establishing good relationships with his peers. Eric felt this was an inaccurate assessment. He feels he works hard to build stakeholder relationships for all of his teammates and shares his presentations freely. When he solves problems, he has the good of the group in mind. He has never felt antagonism from his colleagues. When they travel together for meetings, they always have fun. He thinks his boss is threatened by his good work. She needed to give him a low grade on something so he doesn't outshine her.

Eric approached a colleague who leads a different team to discuss his next steps. With Eric's permission, the colleague first had a conversation with Eric's boss to get her perspective. His boss said Eric had to demonstrate his ability to help other people shine before she will recommend him for a promotion. She didn't think he showed good leadership qualities. Some of his peers appreciate his work, but they don't like the way he boasts and shows off. She has tried to tell him these things, but he either doesn't listen or doesn't respect her opinion.

Themes and Patterns

Although Eric may need to change his behavior, he also needs to improve his relationship with his boss. People who work in organizations are operating within systems. When they act as lone warriors, they create both cheerleaders and enemies. Nelson Mandela said, "If you want to make peace with your enemy, you have to work with your enemy. Then he becomes your partner." It doesn't matter who is right or wrong in this situation. Eric has to determine what he is willing to do to establish a better partnership with the person who currently holds the position as his promoter.

Although trying to mend a damaged relationship seems like the logical choice, people often don't take on this challenge because they feel the loss might be too great. In this case, Eric feels he would be giving in to his manager if he accepts her advice. He feels his personal integrity is at stake. He worries how he will judge himself. His behavior is swayed by his fear without realizing it.

In an alternative scenario, Anna had been offered a new, high-paying job, but she claimed she wasn't ready to move on. She had been a successful team leader and agreed to take on a struggling team to prove she could turn them around. She was on the path to meeting her goal when the offer came in.

After giving me her list of pros and cons, I asked Anna, "Put yourself in both positions successfully a year from now. From that point of view, which one leaves you feeling more regret for not choosing the other?"

She told me about the good work she was doing, but the salary in the new position would give her money for a new house. I repeated my question, "Which decision will leave you with more regret?"

She told me about how she would be leaving the team defenseless, but she would learn so much from the other position. I asked, "So which would leave you with the greatest regret?"

Finally, she said, "I want the new job. I'm just afraid people will say I gave up on my team."

The conversation shifted to how Anna defined *selling out* and if her definitions actually applied to her current scenario. She then explored what doors would open for her and her family if she took the new job. At the end of the conversation, she knew she would have more regrets if she did not take the new position. She also promised herself to reevaluate her choice in one year because she could always move on if the job didn't fulfill her needs.

Choose to explore what holds people back from making the decisions they know are best for them in the long run. The answers often include how other people might judge them or how they might judge themselves if they do what they are resisting. Anna feared negative judgment from others. Eric's pride stood in his way. With the truth on the table, people are better able to make choices that serve their broader needs.

Challenges for the Leader Holding the Conversation (Based on Eric's Situation)

Getting people to disarm their egos can take time. Our brains are well equipped to protect our sense of self and reality. Asking someone to be nicer to the enemy or to do something that others could judge negatively may cause defenses to mount. The best you can do is to keep the focus on the desired outcome in the future. What does the person want? What is he willing to do or put up with to realize his aspirations? Allow him to rant or ramble, but keep the bigger desired outcome in plain sight during the entire conversation.

Debating is futile. When looking at the need to accept negative feedback, the challenge is to refrain from spiraling into a who is right and who is wrong argument. The conversation should stick with the desired outcome in a year or two, taking the decision out of the contentious moment. Then you can look at what is the best thing he can do to achieve the outcome.

Sometimes you need to walk away until he is ready to negotiate. If the person is not willing to take responsibility in changing the dynamics so he can achieve his outcome, then you might share your perception and offer to discuss the situation at another time. If Eric chooses to stay angry with his boss, you can tell him that anger is a normal response in this situation so he can be angry for now. Then when he is ready to brainstorm his next steps, you will resume the conversation. Pushing will only create more resistance. Let the person know you care and are accessible when he is ready to work with you.

Breakthrough Moment

The colleague who was coaching Eric told me he let Eric rant about his situation for a while before asking, "Are you ready to look at what you need to do next or do you need more time to be angry?"

"How do you expect me to respond to an unfair situation?" Eric replied.

"I don't expect anything. I thought you wanted me to help you strategize getting a promotion."

"I do but . . ."

"But the bottom line is you have a boss who may or may not have acted inappropriately. So for now, let's say she did and you have a bad boss. A year from now, do you still want to be angry about your situation or do you want to be in a leadership position?"

"I should be in a leadership position now."

"Maybe. But a year from now, will you regret not doing things differently? Even if you decide to look for another job outside of the company, will you wonder if you could have had the wherewithal to turn this situation around?"

"She will never change."

"What would you like her to do?"

"Listen to me. Trust me more."

"Can you show her how to do that? Could you model great leadership for her?"

That was the moment Eric stopped cold. He pursed his lips and pounded his fist on the chair before he exhaled, releasing the resistance in his body. Finally, he laughed and said, "You got me."

His colleague then asked Eric to look at all the ways he cleverly established relationships with customers and stakeholders. Using his own list, Eric designed a strategy to better manage his relationship with his boss. He said he still felt a little like he was giving in, but in the bigger picture, he was probably learning a good lesson in politics.

Reflection Questions

Have you encountered people like Eric and Anna who are so wrapped up emotionally that they can't see their way forward? What have you done to help clear their view? What would you have done differently in Eric and Anna's cases? Consider these questions on your own or work through them with a colleague or group:

1. What action is the person considering that will leave him with more regrets down the road? Can you help the person visualize his best future so he will be more open to considering something other than what he is doing now?

2. What is his resistance protecting? What judgment is he making about himself, or what does he think others will

say about him if he makes one choice or the other? Don't belittle or discount these statements. The person has to feel comfortable sharing these fears with you so they can be discussed and either discarded or defused.

3. How can the situation be reframed so the choice that feels uncomfortable is considered on par with the easy way out? Keeping the outcome in mind and the fears laid out on the table, the person should be able to see merits of the uncomfortable option. If he decides not to take the uncomfortable path, at least he made the choice consciously instead of emotionally. If your job is to be his thinking partner instead of telling him what to do, then you have done your job well.

Case 3 ■ Been There, Failed That, What's Next?

Background

Lisa is a professional in her forties working for a global corporation. Her team has successfully raised profits and visibility within the entire organization for two years straight. Her boss likes her decisive, direct style. Her peers respect her and her work, but none of them are her friends.

Her boss recently told her that he was recommending she run the Asia Pacific region. This means she will have to move to Hong Kong or Singapore. Whenever she tried to engage her boss in a conversation about the realities of moving to another country, he enthusiastically tells here this is the best opportunity of her career. If she succeeds in this position, which he is sure she will, she can go anywhere in the world, probably for any company in their industry.

Lately, she has showed more emotion in business meetings, getting angry with her peers, and even tearing up in one long afternoon session. Her boss asked her to talk with someone about her outbursts. She contacted me to assess her emotional intelligence.

Lisa told me she has been feeling unmotivated and edgy and can't explain why. She also said she has been stressed about work and not too happy about her life for quite a while. She has even considered leaving her job. She doesn't think her reactions have anything to do with biological changes though she booked an appointment for a physical just to be sure.

In her thirties, Lisa chose to focus on her career at the expense of her social life. She was married, but they grew apart as they both gave more time to their work than to their relationship. After the divorce, Lisa actively dated and had friends until she moved to take her current position at the North American headquarters in San Francisco.

Now in her early forties, Lisa has begun to question her choices. She has had difficulty establishing a social network in San Francisco. She wonders if the work she does is important enough. She has a niggling voice telling her she might have a higher purpose in life if she let herself find it. Maybe there were things she would like to do better if she had the opportunity to try them out, but she has no one to speak with about her concerns.

When her boss gave her the news about his recommendation, she went into a panic. She knew she couldn't say no. Yet she felt she needed time to determine what she wanted for her life before she was consumed with trying to fit into a new culture and living conditions on the other side of the world. His push for a decision is adding stress to her confusion.

Themes and Patterns
Life and professional priorities shift over time. What a person values at one stage in life can shift to look like something else

as he or she grows older. Like Lisa, many people in their forties and fifties question whether there is something else they should consider for their career and whether there is something of greater value they could accomplish. Significance and purpose become more important than titles and money as the major drivers of career choices, especially for high achievers in mid-career.[2]

Although it is normal to periodically assess one's life, the deliberation is difficult to do alone. Increasing isolation is a common occurrence for upwardly mobile high achievers and leaders but rarely discussed or even recognized.[3] Social/emotional support dwindles as they climb the corporate ladder and move away from friends and family for work. Even if they have life partners, they may not feel their partners are suitable sounding boards for work-related topics. As a result, they feel they have no one to talk to about difficult decisions or dilemmas. Their growing loneliness can take a toll on their motivation. When leaders do not help their top performers work through emotional issues, they often lose top talent who seek to find more stable ground elsewhere.

Leaders often miss this need because high achievers often see themselves as self-sufficient and don't seek advice or support from others. They learn fast. They adapt easily. They don't like telling people when they aren't sure of their decisions. Yet like all humans, they need emotional support when the road gets bumpy.

When high achievers need someone to turn to but look around and no one is there, they begin to wonder if their hard work is worth it. Life can feel confining and shallow. They may start looking for something new to do without a plan, not recognizing that external changes won't solve the problem. Without any social/emotional support, Lisa feels she is on shaky ground already. A move to a strange country feels overwhelming.

Additionally, high achievers don't like to fail at anything.[4] Although most high achievers like new challenges that support their growth and provide opportunities to show off their abilities, they avoid projects and changes if there is a risk of failure. Because they have had little experience with failure, they only take on jobs they inherently know they can master. If there is a good shot at success, they will go for the challenge even if it means changing careers and trying something they have never done before. If they don't think they will be able to master the challenge, they will pass. In other words, they won't dance if it makes them look stupid.

For Lisa, the lack of social/emotional support heightened her anxiety about taking the new position, and her manager is making matters worse by not letting her show vulnerability. He doesn't give her a safe space to talk about her concerns. In fact, his flippant answers make her feel as if something is wrong with her. She feels like he is pushing her to the edge of the cliff. Her emotional outbursts are symptoms of the anger and fear she is feeling.

Lisa's manager is missing the opportunity to help her think through the mental swirl in her brain. If she felt his support, she might stay with the company. Right now, the company is at risk of losing one of their best performers.

Challenges for the Leader Holding the Conversation

Hold the space for people to make the right decision whatever that might be. In a Discomfort Zone conversation about difficult decisions, it is important people feel any choice they make is their own. If you try to push them toward one option, they will either try to please you by going along with you or they will shut down, accept your point of view, and leave the conversation disappointed. For people to feel safe enough to openly explore with you, they have to feel you won't judge their ideas. For example, if Lisa decides to go home and live with her mother, that is her choice. No decision is her last. She still has many chapters to live out in her life. When you are in Discomfort Zone conversations, you must stand for the best result for the person you are with whether or not their decision gives you the result you want.

Allowing someone to articulate risks and fears can bring objectivity to her deliberation. There are times people just need to talk things out. I have had executive clients pay me well to act as a sounding board because they have nowhere else to go to weigh their ideas and options. If Lisa had stronger social/emotional support, she might not feel so anxious and confused. You are giving someone a great gift when you listen and facilitate her navigation through risky and troublesome waters.

Maintain the safety bubble no matter what emotions are expressed. If the person expresses fear, anger, or sadness, if there is no threat of harm to you, allow the emotional expression to occur. Do not tell someone, "It will all turn out fine" or "You're smart, you'll figure it out." These comments cut off the conversation. Also, never ask the emotional person if she needs to go somewhere to regroup. This creates embarrassment. Instead, breathe, feel compassion, and wait until the emotion dies down before you ask what feels most important for her to discuss right now. After the emotions are released, the conversation can continue without anyone feeling weak.

Breakthrough Moment

When Lisa realized she was in a supportive conversation with me—that I wasn't going to judge her even if she decided to quit—she was able to talk about her fear that each career move in her life looked good on paper but didn't make her feel so good at the end of the day. This gave me the chance to explore what she needed to do to feel more satisfied with her work and her life.

We started with an easy conversation that allowed her to discover how she could better manage her priorities and increase her energy. We also talked about her trepidation with moving abroad. She determined she could ask her boss if she could do an exploratory trip to Singapore or Hong Kong if she made the final running for the position. This was not an uncommon request for people considering expatriate assignments. If the company wouldn't support this, it was a clear indication of the lack of support she would get from them if she made the move. With this knowledge, she felt better equipped to calculate the level of acceptable risk in her decision.

We then briefly discussed her desire to have a stronger sense of purpose. I gave her some questions to ponder about her mission and purpose before we met again. She knew this process could take time, but she appreciated formal guidance to sort out these complicated questions.

Finally, I asked Lisa, "So what did someone do in your last meeting that made you so angry that you broke down?"

She pressed her lips together and stared at me for a long while before she said. "No one has my back in those meetings. Not my boss. Not my peers."

"Were your boss and peers trying to sabotage you?"

"No. I guess, not consciously."

"Did they know what you needed from them?"

"I thought they would. Maybe I should meet with people before the meetings."

"So you are telling me you had no real reason to be angry?"

"Probably. It's not their fault. I'll say something at the next meeting."

"Tell me Lisa, did you go into the meeting feeling angry?"

"You want me to remember what I was feeling that day?"

"Just before the meeting. Did you go in angry, apprehensive, hopeful . . . ?"

She looked at her hands. "Right now, I'm mad most of the time."

"Who are you mad at?"

She closed her eyes, tipped her head back, and said, "My life sucks. I'm a loser who is soon to be a failure. I can't believe I created this mess." She looked at me and said, "Me, I'm angry at me. I'm angry that no one seems to really care about me and that's my fault."

"Are you ready to do something about that?"

She sighed and said, "It's time I am ready."

In the end, Lisa realized the abyss she felt she was living in was based both on her fear of failing as a human in her midlife and on possibly failing as a professional in her next move. With no one to talk to, she felt the world was closing in on her. Once she quit beating herself up, she determined she needed to rekindle a few friendships and find some time to reflect on what she really wanted for her life.

Reflection Questions

Allow people to tell their full stories so you can hear all the emotions they are feeling. Then use questions like these to explore what, why, and what is next:

1. What is at the source of her anger—unmet expectations, broken promises, or not feeling heard or cared about? What is she longing for? What does she feel has disappeared from her life? What does she need now to move forward? Let the answers surface without judgment. When people become aware of the sources of their

emotions, the answers they seek seem to easily emerge.

2. Does she know why she is on the path she has chosen? Companies have mission statements. People need mission statements as well. They also need to state why this mission is important to them. The *why* becomes the anchor they use when rocked by a big life decision. What about her work and life brings her joy? What is she most proud of? What would she love to be proud of five years from now? Why? Risks become less formidable when people get clear about their higher purpose.

3. Once a person demonstrates her ability to achieve over and over, what's next? What parts of herself did she suppress while she was fixated on achievement? Can she give voice to these parts while doing her current job? The *something more* she seeks will be easier to find when she listens to her inner voice without judgment.

Don't be afraid to lose your employees if you ask these questions; it's likely they will appreciate that you care about them beyond the results they produce. *We all long to be seen and heard.* Discomfort Zone conversations create powerful connections that will serve to strengthen your organization while transforming lives.

Chapter Seven

Strategizing Your Development Plan

"There's only one real sin, and that is to persuade oneself that the second-best is anything but the second-best."

Doris Lessing, *The Golden Notebook*

The last exercise in my leadership classes starts with the question "What will stop you from implementing what you have experienced?" The excuses start with the usual lack of time, pressure to get results, and how they expect their old habits will return. The next layer of excuses includes worrying they will look stupid when trying to coach people so they will fail. Someone will admit to doubting the results. Someone else claims people expect answers from him or her, not questions.

Eventually, someone says that even if she sets goals to practice and courageously move forward, she would be hindered in her development because the culture doesn't support this change. Taking time to develop minds is not recognized as a significant leadership skill. It is trumped by skills such as decisiveness, clear one-way communication, and a more transactional, formulaic, and a consequence-based "whistle around the neck" form of coaching focused on improving performance and winning. Even if she wanted to buck the system, she doesn't feel supported trying to use a skill that takes time to master.

My response to both the personal excuses and the reality around the lack of support is the same question: *Are you willing to do what it takes to realize extraordinary results by changing your conversations?* It takes time to make personal and organizational shifts based on changes in how people think and act. Staying alert to how you handle your interpersonal interactions must be prioritized along with all the other things you have to urgently do. There will be setbacks and disappointments. Your commitment will be tested. You have to keep reminding yourself how proud and satisfied you will feel when you consistently get good results.

There are no shortcuts on the learning curve; you have to regularly use the skills to learn them. There are, however, tips and activities that will help you stick to your goals. First I'll explore ideas you can use for your personal journey. Then I'll share suggestions for increasing acceptance for Discomfort Zone conversations in your organization.

Personal Transformation

The leaders in my classes always agree that they have to deliberately schedule and uphold time for conversations that could turn into Discomfort Zone opportunities. Most say they have to delegate some responsibilities to find the time, say no to meetings and requests that creep into the times they set aside, and above all, not let their own excuses *force* them to reschedule appointments no matter how valid their logic sounds. Making the decision to do what it takes to change habits is easy; *sustaining the commitment on a daily basis* to fully realize the transformation is not easy.

Then they agree to avoid judging themselves when they aren't perfect. Changing habitual behavior patterns can take months of practice and reflection. When you aren't sure what to say and conversations feel uncomfortable, there is safety in returning to old thinking and behaviors. If you stay the course, your skills will become habits and eventually, you will naturally listen more deeply and ask more powerful questions.

When you first try out a new behavior, it may feel awkward and inauthentic. The gap between the old and the new way of being feels uncomfortable. You aren't sure who you are or what you are supposed to do. You might rationalize going back to old behaviors by telling yourself that learning these techniques was a dumb idea. You then abort your commitment to change.

Remember, what feels awkward to you in a Discomfort Zone conversation is actually your brain going through the repatterning process just like what you are hoping will happen for the person you are with. In other words, your discomfort is evidence of positive growth. If you accept your discomfort and settle into the mystery of not knowing what will happen next, you will listen more deeply, allowing the important reflections and questions to emerge. When you accept instead of resist what you are feeling, you ease your personal transformation process.

Seek Support

According to Malcolm Gladwell in his book *Outliers*, successful people do not make it on their own: "No one—not rock stars, not professional athletes, not software billionaires, and not even geniuses—ever makes it alone."[1] Even when your decision to change makes perfect sense and you've decided you want the results enough to work for them, you may fall back into old habits without the right support to help you stay accountable to your goals. There is no need to "tough it out on your own."

Asking for help is a sign of strength, not weakness. If you are truly committed to creating amazing results that impact your workplace and beyond, then you need to access the wisdom and support of others.

Coaches and mentors can help, but your best support will come from a community of colleagues working on similar goals to provide a sounding board and critical eyes to help you stay on track. Gathering a community of support is not a luxury you can put off until you have time someday. Establishing and maintaining your network is a critical step in your growth process.

Coming together with like-minded leaders will keep you from feeling isolated. Empathetic, encouraging colleagues committed to growth can help one another maintain focus when layoffs loom, strategies implode, and projects overwhelm. If you can find people who are consciously trying to become better leaders and uplift their organizations, you can come together to create a positive conspiracy of change.

Creating Your Conspiracies of Change

If you don't have a formal community of support among leaders committed to growth in your company, you can assemble a community using your external networks. Look for like-minded leaders in your professional associations, in executive development classes at your local universities and colleges, and even at your gym. One of my clients, the regional vice president of human resources for a large financial institution, asked her hairdresser to recommend executives from other professions who might want to work on developing their skills and leadership together. As a result, she found six women who welcomed the chance to meet once a month to discuss their goals, obstacles, options, and next steps. They ended each meeting celebrating both large and small wins they experienced the month before. This forced my client to keep a tally of her wins, the evidence of growth she needed to help her stay on course with her goals.

Be clear about your selection criteria for inviting colleagues into your conspiracy. Choose people with positive outlooks who are willing to accept help as well as offer it, who will commit to showing up physically and mentally when you schedule time together, and who are on their own personal development journeys. When you find someone who seems to fit your criteria, ask him to have coffee or a meal with you. When talking, be mindful if he turns every topic into his own story. Instead, look for people who inspire you to trust them through their willingness to share their own concerns and dreams *while having a sincere desire to hear you*rs. You want good listeners who are interested in everyone's growth, not just their own, to build your conspiracy.

If you still can't locate a group to work with, you can find a Discomfort Zone community at http://outsmartyourbrain.com/discomfort-zone-coaching-community/. The web page lists groups who will be sharing cases, answering questions, and practicing skills together. You will also find ongoing learning opportunities to continuously grow your skills on the site.

Celebrate Your Evidence

When you start your Discomfort Zone practice, you must compose easily attainable goals to give your brain the evidence that what you want is achievable. Your brain will revert back to old habits if the changes you are trying to make feel out of reach. To counteract possible disappointment and frustration, you need to frequently experience the feel-good payoff for your personal development work.

From the moment you make the choice to change, determine what you hope to do and achieve in small increments. Then biweekly, if not daily, recognize both the effort and positive effects of your work. Set an intention for your conversations in the morning including how you will stay present and hold positive regard. Then choose to practice one part of the DREAM model or how you maintain trust and safety in the conversation.

At the end of the day, don't focus on what didn't happen. Acknowledge what you did well. Take notes or keep a journal to document the evidence demonstrating you can do what it takes to successfully hold Discomfort Zone conversations. You need to see early and consistent evidence to let your brain know you are capable of success without much distress. Then your brain will align with your goals instead of work against you to keep you from pain.

When you repeatedly appreciate what is positive about your actions, you give reality a chance to unfold before your eyes. You are less likely to get frustrated when you slip and tell someone what *you* think should be done at the start of the conversation or when you judged a person's stories from your head. You override your self-criticism because you also notice when you stepped away from advising and judging, successfully shifting to feeling curious instead. You may have not performed perfectly, but honor yourself for discovering a long-time employee was hurt because of the lack of respect people showed him or a top performer was afraid of people's judgment if she changed her mind about taking a job. The more times you acknowledge the positive effects of your efforts, the quicker the changes will imbed. Then when you meet with your coconspirators, you have victories to share as well as lessons learned.

Your transformation will stay on track if you make a point of noticing your accomplishments every day. Little by little, your efforts become habits. Eventually, you naturally listen more deeply and ask the questions that change minds in your informal as well as scheduled conversations.

Integrate Your Leadership Purpose into Your Conversation Goals

Alfred Adler, one of the founding fathers of psychoanalysis, felt that mental health and development depended on having a life purpose focused on the greater good. A key theme that runs through much of his work is the need to develop social interest based on a sincere "community feeling."[2] If you can tie the changes you want to make to a sense that what you are doing is a part of something bigger than yourself, you are likely to stay consistent with actions needed to achieve your goals. The activist Audre Lorde said, "When I dare to be powerful—to use my strength in the service of my vision—then it becomes less and less important whether I am afraid." *You aren't just achieving goals. You are helping people remove roadblocks in their lives to realize their full potential.* This is your leadership purpose.

A sense of purpose keeps your head above the chaos and negative self-judgment. As mentioned in Chapter Two, you need to set your emotional intention before your conversation, knowing you believe in the other person's potential and your desire is for him to improve, develop, and grow. You are in the conversation for him. You are not there solely because you have goals to meet. Your intention is to use the Discomfort Zone to help people not only see their walls, but to see how their beliefs, defenses, and patterns are limitations hurting their development. You are there to help people create the breakthrough they can't do for themselves because you want the best for them. It is the value you believe you are giving in the moment that will keep you in service of your goals. When you live with this leadership purpose, your excuses for not practicing your skills will have less impact on your choices.

In summary, to ensure success on your personal transformation journey, you need to find a community of support, regularly provide yourself with the evidence of your success, and remind yourself of your leadership purpose to help you stay on track. Even if your journey is delayed, you will be able to stay the course of transformation.

Organizational Transformation

If you believe in the value of *The Discomfort Zone*, you might consider prompting a movement in your organization that will support your own skill development and growth as a leader. A study by Merrill C. Anderson, Chief Business Architect of Cylient, and Candice Frankovelgia and Gina Hernez-Broome, faculty members at The Center for Creative Leadership, identified a growing trend for organizations to use coaching.[3] The study also revealed that the leaders who used coaching in their conversations believed "seismic shifts in performance" were possible if these conversations were imbedded into the organizational culture. There are many resources available outlining what it takes to create a coaching culture in your organization. Anderson, Frankovelgia, and Hemez-Broome's White Paper details a strategy and steps you can use to achieve this desired end. Here are a few tips to help you get started.

Incorporate Discomfort Zone Skills Training into Your Current Leadership Programs

Start by seeing if there is a possibility of adding Discomfort Zone skills training into the current leadership and talent development programs whether these programs already include coaching skills training or not. Because the skills taught in this book offer a specific coaching approach to your conversations not commonly taught or practiced by leaders, you will want to share how these skills differ from what you have been taught before. Find and begin conversations with the stakeholders of these programs in your organization. If there is a passion for developing others and creating leaps in learning and development, you will likely create curiosity if not excitement. You can find tips for trainers and mentor coaches on how to teach the techniques in this book at http://outsmartyourbrain.com/discomfort-zone-training-support/.

As soon as you can, engage top leaders. You can organize special executive sessions where they attend with their peers to learn the skills. You might provide an overview of the book and then review specific case studies as examples of what is possible. Hopefully, the leaders will be curious to learn more. Senior leaders who seek to develop their leadership skills become visible role models and advocates for coaching.

As with any training program, the ideal implementation includes many follow-up activities after the training is held. Here are a few examples:

+ Monthly discussion groups with peers by phone or in person to share successes and coach one another on challenges (internal communities)

+ One-on-one scheduled practice sessions with coaching partners or small groups of three or four people meeting to practice the skills

+ Web-based support materials that are updated regularly

+ Dedicated Discomfort Zone email groups to share ideas and ask questions

+ Regular webinars or follow-up workshops every six months (costly but effective)

Ideally, momentum will build in your organization as more leaders participate and realize success when they implement the skills. Help facilitate acceptance by encouraging early adopters to share their results with others informally. If you formally measure results, be sure to publicize the findings in as many places as possible.

Find a Senior Champion to Link the Skill Development to Business Strategies

If you are not a senior leader, you will need to leverage the authority of someone who is. Proposing changes to what your organization defines as *desired leadership behaviors* requires both data and support. Although it's easy to shoot down one messenger, having an executive lead a flock of messengers is harder to ignore. Discover the person on the executive team who is most known for supporting unconventional and progressive ideas. Court this person with your vision and data.

Prepare your pitch with both numbers and stories that represent the results you have achieved so far. Share your vision of expanding these scenarios to the entire organization. Explain how the shift in leadership style will reinforce succession planning and the retention of engaged workers. If you are courageous enough and the executive is willing, engage him or her in a Discomfort Zone conversation to experience the results firsthand. Hopefully, the conversation will lead to an action plan for pitching the program to the executive team as a way of helping to achieve their priority business goals.

If you and your champion don't win the backing of the executive team in the first round, seek to align your program with next year's business strategies. "When initiatives to create coaching cultures are viewed as business initiatives rather than as just learning and development initiatives, continued investment and senior-leader support are strengthened and sustained," said

Cylient principal Merrill Anderson.[4] Remember that changing the culture isn't an event; it's a long-term process that should tie into the strategies for accelerating human capability.

Advocating for this change takes persistence and courage, just as you need to do for your personal transformation. As demonstrated in the examples and cases in this book, the rewards are well worth the investment. Leading in the Discomfort Zone is where the magic happens.

CHAPTER SEVEN: Key Points to Remember

1. You have to override personal and organizational resistance to sustain changes in your leadership style.

2. Discomfort Zone conversations will feel awkward at first. This is evidence you are repatterning your own brain. Settle into the mystery of not knowing to facilitate your growth.

3. Find or create your own positive conspiracies of change. Trying to succeed on your own is much harder than when you have a community of support to practice with, exchange ideas, and share successes.

4. Regularly provide yourself with evidence of your successes and remind yourself of your leadership purpose to sustain your development.

5. If you want to create a movement in your organization, link Discomfort Zone skills training to business and succession planning strategies. Then seek to integrate the training into current leadership programs. Find senior leaders to champion your plans. The rewards are worth the investment.

Notes

Introduction: What Is Good about Discomfort?

1. Joseph Jaworski. *Synchronicity: The Inner Path of Leadership.* Berrett-Koehler, 1996. The description of how Jaworski defines *true leadership* is on page 2 of the introduction, written by Peter Senge.

2. Michael Gazzaniga. *Who's in Charge: Free Will and the Science of the Brain.* Ecco, 2011, page 43.

3. Ibid., page 67.

4. Srinivasan S. Pillay. *Your Brain and Business: The Neuroscience of Great Leaders.* FT Press, 2011, pages 132–137.

5. Daniel Kahneman, *Thinking, Fast and Slow.* Farrar, Straus & Giroux, 2011. Kahneman describes what happens when thinking is disrupted and new perception forms on pages 24, 33, 51, 89, and 174.

6. Joshua Fields Millburn and Ryan Nicodemus, *The Discomfort Zone.* The Minimalists blog at www.theminimalists.com/zone/.

7. Monika Hamori, Jie Cao, and Burak Koyuncu. "Why Top Young Managers Are in a Nonstop Job Hunt." *Harvard Business Review*, July 1, 2012. Retrieved from http://hbr.org/2012/07/why-top-young-managers-are-in-a-nonstop-job-hunt/.

Chapter One: Criteria for Choosing a Discomfort Zone Conversation

1. James Showkeir and Maren Showkeir. *Authentic Conversations: Moving from Manipulation to Truth and Commitment*. Berrett-Koehler, 2008.

2. Kerry Patterson, Joseph Grenny, Ron McMillan, and Al Switzler. *Crucial Conversations: Tools for Talking When Stakes Are High*. The first edition was released in 2002. A second edition was released by McGraw-Hill, 2013.

3. Ralph Nader. *Crashing the Party*. St. Martin's Press, 2002.

4. Ron Ashkenas and Lisa Bodell. "Nice Managers Embrace Conflict, Too," HBR blog. October 2013. Retrieved from http://blogs.hbr.org/2013/10/nice-managers-embrace-conflict-too/.

5. Malcolm Gladwell. *Blink: The Power of Thinking without Thinking*. Little Brown, 2005, page 71. Aronson referred to numerous studies that demonstrate this phenomenon.

6. Tori Rodriguez. "Taking the Bad with the Good," *Scientific American Mind*. May/June 2013, pages 26–27.

7. Geoffrey James, "8 Core Beliefs of Extraordinary Bosses." Inc.com, April 23, 2012. The beliefs alluded to here are, "A company is a community, not a machine" and "My employees are my peers, not my children." Retrieved from www.inc.com/geoffrey-james/8-core-beliefs-of-extraordinary-bosses.html.

8. Daniel Pink. *Drive: The Surprising Truth About What Motivates Us*. Riverhead Books, 2011. Pink defines the top three motivators as *Autonomy*: People want to have control over their work; *Mastery*: People want to get better at what they do; and *Purpose*: People want to be part of something that is bigger than they are.

9. The description of the Hero's Journey is adapted from: Joseph Campbell. *The Hero with a Thousand Faces*. Princeton University Press, 1968, page 245.

Chapter Two: What Comes First

1. In his book, *Modern Man in Search of a Soul* (translated to English in 1933, Kegan Paul, Trench, Trubner & Co. First publication by Routledge Press, 2001, page 49), Carl Jung said, "The meeting of two personalities is like the contact of two chemical substances: if there is any reaction, both are transformed." He was describing the effects of thoughts and emotions in a doctor-patient relationship. The phenomenon can be applied to any human interaction.

2. Michael Gazzaniga. *Who's in Charge: Free Will and the Science of the Brain*. Ecco, 2011, page 136.

3. Siyuan Liu. "Neural Correlates of Lyrical Improvisation: An fMRI Study of Freestyle Rap," *Scientific Reports* 2:834. November 15, 2012.

4. Psychologist Mihaly Csikszentmihalyi has spent decades researching times when people become so involved in an activity that nothing else seems to matter; they are in the zone of doing with minimal thoughts and no sense of time. He called this phenomenon "flow." His book that introduced the concept is *Flow: The Psychology of Optimal Experience*. HarperCollins, 1990. Significant research has now been done by others to define this mental state and how to create it.

5. Martin Buber, translated by Walter Kaufmann. *I and Thou*. Touchstone, 1971.

6. Margaret Wheatly. *Leadership and the New Science* (2nd ed.). Berrett-Koehler, November 1999.

7. Daniel Goleman. *Social Intelligence: The New Science of Human Relationships*. Bantam, October, 2006, page 42.

8. A list of emotional triggers plus tips on how to recognize when they are affecting your conversations can be found in: Marcia Reynolds. *Outsmart Your Brain*. Covisioning, 2004, pages 28–31.

Chapter Three: The Map and the Milestones for Your Conversation

1. Special thanks to D. J. Mitsch and the Pyramid Resource Group for helping to formulate the foundational elements of the DREAM process. The Deep Dive model they use to teach organizational coaches worldwide brings to light the critical elements you must listen for to achieve breakthroughs in thinking: story and truth, both as emerging and evolving concepts.

2. Jonathan Gottschall. *The Storytelling Animal: How Stories Make Us Human*. Houghton Mifflin Harcourt, 2012.

Chapter Four: How to Listen for What to Say

1. Daniel Kahneman. *Thinking Fast and Slow*. Penguin, 2012.

2. Sir Arthur Conan Doyle. "A Scandal in Bohemia," *The Adventures of Sherlock Holmes*. 1892.

3. David Dotlich, Peter Cairo, and Stephen Rhinesmith. *Head, Heart & Guts: How the World's Best Companies Develop Complete Leaders*. Jossey-Bass, 2006.

4. Michael Gershon. *The Second Brain: A Groundbreaking New Understanding of Nervous Disorders of the Stomach and Intestine*. Harper, 1998.

5. The HeartMath Institute continues to expand on Dr. Armour's findings as they research and teach people how to access the heart's intelligence to release stress, be more resilient, and succeed in life. You can read more at www.heartmath.org and access an article on heart intelligence incorporating Dr. Armour's work at http://www.heartmath.org/free-services/articles-of-the-heart/index.html.

6. Grant Soosalu and Marvin Oka. "Neuroscience and the Three Brains of Leadership," www.MBraining.com, 2012. You can read the article at http://www.mbraining.com/mbit-and-leadership. A

number of the exercises in this chapter were adapted from their work accessing "the three brains" to make better decisions and to listen more deeply to others.

7. Marc-André Reinhard, Rainer Greifeneder, and Martin Scharmach, "Unconscious processes improve lie detection," *Journal of Personality and Social Psychology*, 105(5):721–739, November 2013.

8. Martin Bos and Amy Cuddy. *Is your iPhone Turning You into a Wimp?* Harvard Business School Working Knowledge. Retrieved from http://hbswk.hbs.edu/ on June 24, 2013.

Chapter Five: New Perspective—Using Discomfort Zone Conversations to Break Through Barriers

1. The European School of Management and Technology continues to hold Coaching Colloquiums every year. You can find more information at http://www.esmt.org/faculty-research/center-and-chairs/center-leadership-development-research-cldr/esmt-coaching.

2. Konstantin Korotov, Elizabeth Florent-Treacy, Manfred F.R. Kets de Vries, and Andreas Bernhardt. *Tricky Coaching: Difficult Cases in Leadership Coaching*. Palgrave Macmillan, 2012.

3. The Healthcare Coaching Institute teaches organizational leaders and coaches who want to learn deep coaching skills and seek certification by the International Coach Federation. You can find more information at http://pyramidresource.com/healthcarecoachinginstitute.

4. Scott Eblin. *The Next Level: What Insiders Know About Executive Success*. Davies-Black, 2006, page 137.

5. Typical behavioral patterns of high-achieving women are detailed in: Marcia Reynolds. *Wander Woman: How High-Achieving Women Find Contentment and Direction*. Berrett-Koehler, 2010, pages 76–82.

6. William Bridges. *Transitions: Making Sense of Life's Changes* (2nd ed.). Da Capo Press, 2004.

Chapter Six: Transformation—Using Discomfort Zone Conversations to Embrace What's Next

1. James MacGregor Burns first defined the two leadership styles. He said transactional leaders focus on goals, rewards, and punishment based on results and loyalty. Transformational leaders engage with followers, focus on higher-order intrinsic needs, and raise consciousness to see new ways in which outcomes might be achieved. They listen for the beliefs, needs, and values of their followers and prefer conversations instead of directions. You can read more in his classic book, *Leadership*. HarperCollins, 1978.

2. Connie Gersick and Kathy Kram. "High-Achieving Women at Mid-Life: An Exploratory Study," *Journal of Management Inquiry* II, June 2002:104–127. It is becoming more common for men to experience similar phases as well.

3. Psychologist Guy Winch, author of *Emotional First Aid* (Hudson Street Press, 2013), wrote a blog post on social/emotional isolation and leadership for SwitchandShift.com called *Lonely at the Top: Why Good Leaders Must Learn to Manage Loneliness*, August 29, 2013. Retrieved from http://switchandshift.com/lonely-at-the-top-why-good-leaders-must-learn-to-manage-loneliness.

4. Common blindspots and behavioral patterns of high-achieving women are detailed in Marcia Reynolds. *Wander Woman: How High-Achieving Women Find Contentment and Direction*. Berrett-Koehler, 2010, pages 71–82. There are many men who also exhibit these patterns.

Chapter Seven: Strategizing Your Development Plan

1. Malcolm Gladwell, *Outliers: The Story of Success*. Little Brown, 2008, page 115.

2. Alfred Adler. *Social Interest: A Challenge to Mankind*. Oneworld Publications, 1998, pages 2–3.

3. The study is featured in the Center for Creative Leadership (CCL) White Paper, *Creating Coaching Cultures: What Business Leaders Expect and Strategies to Get There*. January 2009.

4. Merrill Anderson. *Bottom-Line Organization Development*. Butterworth-Heinemann, 2003. Center for Creative Leadership (CCL) White Paper, *Creating Coaching Cultures: What Business Leaders Expect and Strategies to Get There*. January 2009.

Acknowledgments

To this day, I am grateful every time a colleague shares my work. You may not be named here, but know I am thankful beyond words for your support. I am lucky to know you.

I am indebted to Neal Mallet, my editor, for hearing the kernels of my ideas and directing me on a coherent path. His wisdom kept my focus. His feedback was always right on. May he always have the courage to share what is on his mind!

I am in awe of my vast global coaching community, for the friendships and the learning I receive from my colleagues. D. J. Mitsch, president of the Pyramid Resource Group, had the courage and foresight to found the Healthcare Coaching Institute and appoint me the training director. Designing the training for the program helped me codify the skills and write this book. Then Harriet Simon Salinger helped make sure the heart and soul of the work remained intact. Without this experience, the book would not exist.

Zoran Todorovic, president of TNM Coaching, opened many possibilities for my work on a global level. He, too, has given me a tribe of coaches who are dedicated to transforming the world. I will wake up at any hour to meet and conspire with the TNM team.

To my cheerleaders: Vickie Sullivan, you are my most constant source of support. Thanks to Hayley Foster, I have a core message. Thanks to Lili Xu Brandt, Svetlana Chumakova, Toni Koch, Linda Lunden, Sherri Kilian, Paul Jantzi, Eve Clark, Wendy White, Dennece McKelvy, and Megan McCoy. And thanks to all my clients over the years. This book is about what I learned from you.

Above all, I am grateful with all my heart for Karl Schnell, my life partner. He unconditionally supports me and my work even when I am called to travel thousands of miles away. He then gives me the space to write when I return. As I continue to learn how to open my heart, Karl is my greatest teacher. The gratitude I feel for everything deepens because of Karl.

Index

Index

trust, 16, 21, 27, 30–33
of the process, 37–41

U
unity, 35

V
values, personal, 21
Van Gogh, Vincent, 38–39
venting, 90–91
vision, 20

visualization, 68, 76, 80
vulnerability, 4, 32

W
walls of protection, 9
Ward, William Arthur, 87
"what" questions, 58
Wheatley, Margaret, 35
Whitmore, John, 13
willingness to talk, 21
worst case scenarios, 20

About the Author

Dr. Marcia Reynolds works with clients around the world who seek to develop effective leaders. She understands organizational cultures, especially what blocks communication and innovation and what is needed to bring people together for better results. She has coached leaders, taught leadership and coaching classes, and spoken at conferences in thirty-four countries. She has more than thirty years of experience in organizational training and development with more than twenty years as an executive coach.

In her last corporate position, Marcia's greatest success story came as a result of designing the employee development program for a semiconductor manufacturing company facing bankruptcy. Working with the executive staff, Marcia focused on improving leadership communication and empowering cross-functional teams to become the heart of the organization. The company turned around and became the top performing IPO in the United States in 1993.

Excerpts from her previous books, *Outsmart Your Brain* and *Wander Woman: How High Achieving Women Find Contentment and Direction*, have appeared in many places including *Harvard Management Review, Employment Relations Today, Forbes.com, CNN*.

com, *Psychology Today*, and numerous business publications in Europe and Asia, and she has appeared on *ABC World News*.

For coaching, Marcia works with both individuals and executive teams. Individually, she is often asked to coach leaders who technically excel but seek to develop their interpersonal effectiveness. After working with Marcia, her clients demonstrate remarkable improvements in engaging their teams and mastering influence with their peers and senior leaders.

Marcia is a true pioneer of the global coaching profession. She was the fifth global president of the International Coach Federation and one of the first twenty-five people in the world to earn the Master Certified Coach designation. She is the training director for the Healthcare Coaching Institute and has been a board member of the Association for Coach Training Schools. She has helped start coaching schools in Russia and China and continues to speak at coaching conferences around the world.

Marcia's doctoral degree is in organizational psychology with a research focus on high achievers in today's corporations. She holds two masters degrees, one in education and the other in communications.

In her rare spare time, she can be found hiking the beautiful mountains near her home in Arizona.

Find out more about Marcia's programs at

www.outsmartyourbrain.com

Also by Marcia Reynolds

Wander Woman

How High-Achieving Women Find Contentment and Direction

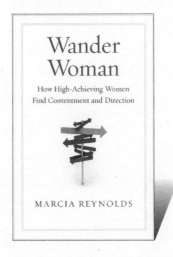

There is a new generation of high-achieving women: confident, ambitious, and driven yet impatient, discontented, and, above all, restless. Constantly juggling multiple roles and reevaluating goals, today's "wander women" move from job to job, challenge to challenge, almost on impulse. Drawing on fresh research and extensive interviews, Marcia Reynolds helps you understand the roots of your restlessness and discover how to make your wandering a conscious strategy, not a series of unplanned events. She provides a wealth of exercises and practices so you can better understand the needs that drive your decisions, discover new ways of finding direction, and thoughtfully choose and plan your future—whether climbing the corporate ladder, finding satisfaction below the glass ceiling, or setting out on your own.

Paperback, 264 pages, ISBN 978-1-60509-351-2
PDF ebook, ISBN 978-1-60509-353-6

BK® Berrett–Koehler Publishers, Inc.
San Francisco, *www.bkconnection.com*

800.929.2929

Berrett–Koehler
Publishers

Berrett-Koehler is an independent publisher dedicated to an ambitious mission: *Creating a World That Works for All*.

We believe that to truly create a better world, action is needed at all levels—individual, organizational, and societal. At the individual level, our publications help people align their lives with their values and with their aspirations for a better world. At the organizational level, our publications promote progressive leadership and management practices, socially responsible approaches to business, and humane and effective organizations. At the societal level, our publications advance social and economic justice, shared prosperity, sustainability, and new solutions to national and global issues.

A major theme of our publications is "Opening Up New Space." Berrett-Koehler titles challenge conventional thinking, introduce new ideas, and foster positive change. Their common quest is changing the underlying beliefs, mindsets, institutions, and structures that keep generating the same cycles of problems, no matter who our leaders are or what improvement programs we adopt.

We strive to practice what we preach—to operate our publishing company in line with the ideas in our books. At the core of our approach is stewardship, which we define as a deep sense of responsibility to administer the company for the benefit of all of our "stakeholder" groups: authors, customers, employees, investors, service providers, and the communities and environment around us.

We are grateful to the thousands of readers, authors, and other friends of the company who consider themselves to be part of the "BK Community." We hope that you, too, will join us in our mission.

A BK Business Book

This book is part of our BK Business series. BK Business titles pioneer new and progressive leadership and management practices in all types of public, private, and nonprofit organizations. They promote socially responsible approaches to business, innovative organizational change methods, and more humane and effective organizations.

Berrett–Koehler
Publishers

A community dedicated to creating
a world that works for all

Dear Reader,

Thank you for picking up this book and joining our worldwide community of Berrett-Koehler readers. We share ideas that bring positive change into people's lives, organizations, and society.

To welcome you, we'd like to offer you a free e-book. You can pick from among twelve of our bestselling books by entering the promotional code **BKP92E** here: http://www.bkconnection.com/welcome.

When you claim your free e-book, we'll also send you a copy of our e-newsletter, the *BK Communiqué*. Although you're free to unsubscribe, there are many benefits to sticking around. In every issue of our newsletter you'll find

- A free e-book
- Tips from famous authors
- Discounts on spotlight titles
- Hilarious insider publishing news
- A chance to win a prize for answering a riddle

Best of all, our readers tell us, "Your newsletter is the only one I actually read." So claim your gift today, and please stay in touch!

Sincerely,

Charlotte Ashlock
Steward of the BK Website

Questions? Comments? Contact me at bkcommunity@bkpub.com.